WORKING UNDER THE SAFETY NET

SAGE HUMAN SERVICES GUIDES, VOLUME 47

SAGE HUMAN SERVICES GUIDES

a series of books edited by ARMAND LAUFFER and CHARLES D. GARVIN.
Published in cooperation with the University of Michigan School of Social
Work and other organizations.

1: **GRANTSMANSHIP** by Armand Lauffer
(second edition)
2: **CREATING GROUPS** by Harvey J. Bertcher and
Frank F. Maple
4: **SHARED DECISION MAKING**
by Frank F. Maple
5: **VOLUNTEERS** by Armand Lauffer and
Sarah Gorodezky with Jay Callahan and
Carla Overberger
7: **FINDING FAMILIES** by Ann Hartman
8: **NO CHILD IS UNADOPTABLE**
edited by Sallie R. Churchill,
Bonnie Carlson, and Lynn Nybell
9: **HEALTH NEEDS OF CHILDREN**
by Roger Manela and Armand Lauffer with
Eugene Feingold and Ruben Meyer
10: **GROUP PARTICIPATION** by Harvey J. Bertcher
11: **BE ASSERTIVE** by Sandra Stone Sundel and
Martin Sundel
12: **CHILDREN IN CRISIS**
by Carmie Thrasher Cochrane and
David Voit Myers
14: **NEEDS ASSESSMENT** by Keith A. Neuber with
William T. Atkins, James A. Jacobson, and
Nicholas A. Reuterman
15: **DEVELOPING CASEWORK SKILLS**
by James A. Pippin
16: **MUTUAL HELP GROUPS**
by Phyllis R. Silverman
17: **EFFECTIVE MEETINGS** by John E. Tropman
19: **USING MICROCOMPUTERS IN SOCIAL
AGENCIES** by James B. Taylor
20: **CHANGING ORGANIZATIONS AND
COMMUNITY PROGRAMS** by Jack Rothman,
John L. Erlich, and Joseph G. Teresa
21: **MATCHING CLIENTS AND SERVICES**
by R. Mark Mathews and Stephen B. Fawcett
22: **WORKING WITH CHILDREN** by Dana K. Lewis
23: **MAKING DESEGREGATION WORK**
by Mark A. Chesler, Bunyan I. Brant, and
James E. Crowfoot
24: **CHANGING THE SYSTEM** by Milan J. Dluhy
25: **HELPING WOMEN COPE WITH GRIEF**
by Phyllis R. Silverman
26: **GETTING THE RESOURCES YOU NEED**
by Armand Lauffer
27: **ORGANIZING FOR COMMUNITY ACTION**
by Steve Burghardt
28: **AGENCIES WORKING TOGETHER**
by Robert J. Rossi, Kevin J. Gilmartin, and
Charles W. Dayton

29: **EVALUATING YOUR AGENCY'S
PROGRAMS** by Michael J. Austin, Gary Cox,
Naomi Gottlieb, J. David Hawkins,
Jean M. Kruzich, and Ronald Rauch
30: **ASSESSMENT TOOLS** by Armand Lauffer
31: **UNDERSTANDING PROGRAM
EVALUATION** by Leonard Rutman and
George Mowbray
32: **UNDERSTANDING SOCIAL NETWORKS**
by Lambert Maguire
33: **FAMILY ASSESSMENT** by Adele M. Holman
34: **THE ACCOUNTABLE AGENCY**
by Reginald Carter
35: **SUPERVISION** by Eileen Gambrill and
Theodore J. Stein
36: **BUILDING SUPPORT NETWORKS FOR
THE ELDERLY** by David C. Biegel,
Barbara K. Shore, and Elizabeth Gordon
37: **STRESS MANAGEMENT FOR HUMAN
SERVICES** by Richard E. Farmer,
Lynn Hunt Monahan, and Reinhold W. Hekeler
38: **FAMILY CAREGIVERS AND DEPENDENT
ELDERLY** by Dianne Springer and
Timothy H. Brubaker
39: **DESIGNING AND IMPLEMENTING
PROCEDURES FOR HEALTH AND
HUMAN SERVICES** by Morris Schaefer
40: **GROUP THERAPY WITH ALCOHOLICS**
by Baruch Levine and Virginia Gallogly
41: **DYNAMIC INTERVIEWING** by Frank F. Maple
42: **THERAPEUTIC PRINCIPLES IN PRACTICE**
by Herbert S. Strean
43: **CAREERS, COLLEAGUES, AND CONFLICTS**
by Armand Lauffer
44: **PURCHASE OF SERVICE CONTRACTING**
by Peter M. Kettner and Lawrence L. Martin
45: **TREATING ANXIETY DISORDERS**
by Bruce A. Thyer
46: **TREATING ALCOHOLISM**
by Norman K. Denzin
47: **WORKING UNDER THE SAFETY NET**
by Steve Burghardt and Michael Fabricant
48: **MANAGING HUMAN SERVICES
PERSONNEL** by Peter J. Pecora and
Michael J. Austin
49: **IMPLEMENTING CHANGE IN SERVICE
PROGRAMS** by Morris Schaefer

A **SAGE** HUMAN SERVICES GUIDE 47

WORKING UNDER THE SAFETY NET
Policy and Practice with the New American Poor

Steve BURGHARDT
Michael FABRICANT

*Published in cooperation with the University of
Michigan School of Social Work*

SAGE PUBLICATIONS
Newbury Park   Beverly Hills   London   New Delhi

Copyright © 1987 by Sage Publications, Inc.

For information address:

SAGE Publications, Inc.
2111 West Hillcrest Drive
Newbury Park, California 91320

SAGE Publications Inc.
275 South Beverly Drive
Beverly Hills
California 90212

SAGE Publications Ltd.
28 Banner Street
London EC1Y 8QE
England

SAGE PUBLICATIONS India Pvt. Ltd.
M-32 Market
Greater Kailash I
New Delhi 110 048 India

Printed in the United States of America

Library of Congress Cataloging-in-Publication Data

Burghardt, Stephen.
    Working under the safety net.

    (Sage human services guides ; v. 47)
    Includes bibliographical references.
    1. Poor--United States. 2. United States—
Social Policy. 3. Public welfare—United States.
I. Fabricant, Michael.   Title.
HC110.P6B88   1987   362.5'0973   86-27970
ISBN 0-8039-2700-2 (pbk.)

CONTENTS

Acknowledgments   6

Introduction   7

1. The Recent Intensification of Poverty   11

2. Homelessness   23

3. The Hungry   48

4. Older Americans   73

5. Black, Single-Parent Women   91

6. The Physically Disabled   113

7. The New Unemployed   139

8. From Under the Safety Net to Empowerment: New Organizational and Practice Directions for the 1990s   156

References   175

About the Authors   180

ACKNOWLEDGMENTS

We would like to thank the following people for their substantial contributions to this book. We start with Armand Lauffer for his timely editorial comments; Mimi Abramovitz, Rebecca Donovan, Terry Mizrahi, and Rino Patti of the Hunter College School of Social Work; Edie Chency, Bill Crum, Bernice Davis, Joan Driscoll, Jacinta Fernandes, Jeanette Gilbert, Eddie Gray, Peter Liquori, and Sue Marcus of the Elizabeth Coalition to House the Homeless; Ed Allen (Corporate Campaign, Inc.), Judy Hermann (Berkeley Center for Independent Living), Allan Kahan (formerly N.Y. Food and Hunger Hotline), Michael Kelly (Bowery Residential Committee), Naomi Schott (Gray Panthers), Ann Schwartzman (Philadelphia Unemployment Project), Jim Weissman (Eastern Paralyzed Veterans Association) and Scott Smith (HCSSW student). Needless to say special thanks must be extended to our families, Betsy Fabricant, Paula Kramer, Josh, Lila, Matt, and Niki.

Dedicated with love and respect to

the late Steve Zeluck (1922-1985), a man of unbending principle and unwavering belief in the rights and dignity of working people, and

Jacinta Fernandes, who, by example, daily instructs on the true meaning of empowerment, courage, integrity.

INTRODUCTION

If ever there were a country where there should be no poor, it is the United States of America. With a Gross National Product in the trillions, 70% of the largest economic corporations in the world, and its overabundance of foodstuffs found in warehouses throughout its agricultural heartland, America is indeed rich. But it is also poor. The federal debt, too, is well over a trillion dollars; American corporations have let go 18% of their 1973 workforce as they struggle to remain competitive in a leaner, more capital-intensive world economy; and the overabundant heartland faces the largest number of farm foreclosures since the 1930s.

This book is about the poor America, one that in fact "has always been with us," but one also different in its form and much of its content than that of the past. Most of the poor have always served as a reserve pool of labor for the American economy, entering it in robust times, forced to leave it in lean.[1] This classical economic and social function continues its present role in determining the fate of the poor. It will be touched on in various chapters of the book. But many of the poor of late twentieth-century America have been affected also by the particular dynamics of the welfare state, especially since its drastic overhaul begun under the Carter administration and greatly intensified under Ronald Reagan in the 1980s.

Some of these poor have been on welfare for years and perhaps view it in dependent ways that are coming to distress progressives and liberals. Others need social services and entitlements only at old age and view their new status with shame, others with fear. And there are many poor who have never been in need before and do not understand why in their most productive years they are unable to find work.

Conforming to classical functions in many ways, these American poor are yet often distinguishable in their needs, expectations, and service interests today. But they, and the human-service workers who work with them, are joined together by a further dynamic common to late twentieth-century America: a welfare state whose rate of growth is diminishing, not increasing. The corresponding strains created by this falling rate of growth, when coupled with the distinct needs of today's American poor, have led to as much variation in practice delivery as in any other time in American social-welfare history.

Working Under The Safety Net: Policy and Practice with the New American Poor examines these issues. For some, the welfare state appears a blessing; more entitlements and benefits are available now than at any time in American history. For others, working or trapped inside it, the net looks down at them like a web, ensnaring them in bureaucratic red tape and social stigma that makes their poverty even more painful. Recognizing these shifting perceptions, this book is designed with three purposes. The first is straightforward: to critically analyze the dimensions of American poverty and to present the forms of service intervention recently created to work with, and advocate, the poor. Each chapter will explore the arguments surrounding the existence and relative poverty facing each group. For example, there are sharply varying opinions today about the degree of hunger, the causes of homelessness, and the amount of welfare dependence. This descriptive overview will synthesize the discussion surrounding each poor group so that interested professionals and activists will have access to pertinent points of view on each subject.

Second, we will review the forms of intervention that have sprung up so that others, if they wish, can replicate or modify them for their own communities' use. For example, there were few "new unemployed" before 1975; there had been few unemployed councils or utility rate freeze campaigns since the Great Depression. Knowing the forms of intervention and the lessons of various types of advocacy (which will range from individual case advocacy to organizing such as the above-mentioned utility rate-freeze campaign) can simplify other service workers' efforts in the future.

There is also a third objective to this work. By examining the concrete forms of service and the particular needs of the American poor, we also will be critiquing, for better *and* for worse, the present welfare state and its policies. For example, there is new evidence emanating from important black organizations such as the

Urban League that some of the ways in which welfare grants have been distributed may have served to undermine the structure of the poor urban black families. On the other hand, Medicare, while not addressing long-term care needs at all, has served to prolong and improve life for many senior citizens.

We will use this critique in combination with the description of new service innovations among the poor to outline the direction of progressive change that needs to occur throughout the welfare state if human-service workers and their allies are to move out of the defensive posture in which they now find themselves. While this latter discussion will form much of the last chapter, it is integral to any of the specifics undertaken among particular groups of the American poor. It is important, as Santayana said, to learn the lessons of the past so that we are not doomed to repeat them. The tremendous urgency that human-service workers feel to help the homeless, feed the hungry, and assist the increasingly impoverished disabled should not blind them to the responsibility to create services that not only help individuals but carry within them the seeds of lasting change. For only such change can permanently diminish the oppressive conditions experienced by the poor.

This book is designed to meet these three objectives in a simple and accessible form. The first chapter presents an overview of the economic and social landscape of the United States that has created the American poor of late twentieth-century America. Unlike the chapters that follow, it will emphasize the apparent causes of poverty today, examining how and why political and policy choices have helped create the conditions that the poor now face. Chapters 2 through 7 look at the particular subgroups of the poor: the homeless, the hungry, the single-parent mother on AFDC, the physically disabled, poor seniors, the new unemployed. At times, parts of each group will overlap with another. However, each group, its problems, and the forms of service intervention are varied enough to warrant distinctive treatment. At the end of each chapter will be appendices, checklists, and sets of procedures for the reader to use to begin establishing equivalent services in her or his area. The last chapter will summarize the service and policy implications of working with the American poor today. It will also identify a process of empowerment and program/agency building that has structural implications for reform within the welfare state.

Unlike most other Human Service guides' lists and appendices, the end-chapter materials lack uniformity in their headings and suggestions for intervention, etc. This variability reflects the distinctiveness each group warrants, with advocacy and services being highly developed for some, much more preliminary for others.

NOTE

1. The best American interpretation of this phenomenon remains Frances Fox Piven and Richard Cloward's *Regulating the Poor*. See especially chapters 1 and 2.

Chapter 1

THE RECENT INTENSIFICATION OF POVERTY

THE PROBLEM

Newspaper headlines constantly remind us that despite pronouncements of economic recovery, large numbers of Americans are falling over the abyss into the most acute forms of poverty witnessed in this country since the Great Depression. Marked increases in homelessness, hunger, and chronic unemployment among former blue-collar workers and minority youth have not abated, but rather have expanded substantially in the 1980s. For example, 15.2% of all Americans under 18 presently live in poverty as compared to 14.3% in 1969-1970 (Bureau of the Census, 1984). Just as important, the circumstances of other vulnerable groups such as the elderly, female-headed families and the physically disabled have deteriorated significantly during this period. Today, 53% of all black Americans in single-headed families live in poverty as compared to 39.6% in 1969 (Joe and Rogers, 1985). Too often this rapid intensification of poverty has been defined as isolated (albeit persistent and expanding) pockets of misery and not associated with the larger economy.

In part this is a consequence of the manner in which homelessness, hunger, and the new unemployed have come to public consciousness in the 1980s. In effect, the complex social, political, and economic variables that account for the recent intensification of poverty have been reduced to moral formulations fashioned centuries ago. The physical and emotional deterioration associated with homelessness, recent unemployment, or hunger is described by

11

many who are sincerely concerned about these problems as a moral affront in a land as affluent as the United States. The immediate, and for many, long-term responses to this circumstance have been to create shelters or soup lines and, perhaps just as significantly, recreate the "gift relationship" of services, which defines the worthy poor or homeless, disabled, hungry, and recently unemployed, as passive, grateful, and spiritually saint-like (Stern, 1984). Finally, this perspective has tended to emphasize the responsibility of private individuals and church groups in any overarching plan that is intended to affect positively this circumstance. In effect, church groups are expected to use their resources to develop shelters, soup lines, jobs, and the like, and thus establish a partnership with the public sector. This initiative has emerged in part out of the frustration of public officials who have, for instance, seen the contradictory outcomes of geometric expansion in soup lines and shelters concurrent with the demand for more facilities continuing unabated. This call can also be traced to the presumption that individuals must make such personal and moral choices if the struggle against poverty is to be successful (New York Times, December 4, 1984).

These trends in part reflect the ongoing reduction of the public sector's role in addressing or resolving social problems. These moral invectives and the currently modest policy initiatives perhaps represent critical first steps in developing a strong constituent group for those citizens who are increasingly falling below the "safety net." Ultimately, this grouping, however, will have to develop an analysis and agenda that both adequately explains the recent intensification of poverty and has the potential to develop some long- and short-term policies that meet the constellation of needs of these citizens.

In the pages that follow we will develop a preliminary sketch of the relationship between the political and economic landscape and the intensification of poverty. In our analysis we will be particularly concerned with explaining the response of the welfare state and the larger social order to the homeless, hungry, physically disabled, elderly poor, female-headed families, and recently unemployed within the context of a crisis in the marketplace. The first section of each chapter specifically examines the relationship between the fiscal crisis and marketplace wage reductions. This discussion will establish a context for explaining the dramatic decline(s) in the real value of the social wage (a basement income available to Americans through entitlements such as Aid for Families with Dependent Children [AFDC], Social Security Insurance [SSI], food stamps, and unemployment insurance) and the intensification of poverty.

THE CRISIS IN THE MARKETPLACE
AND THE REDUCTION OF WAGES

The seeds of the present growth in poverty were sown during the 1970s. This decade was marked by the most acute expressions of economic crisis since the 1930s. Investment decisions, private savings, and weekly paychecks were affected by sustained bouts with double-digit inflation. The nation witnessed the loss of approximately 30 million jobs during this period. As Bluestone and Harrison have documented (1982), by 1976 plant shutdowns had wiped out 39% of the jobs that existed in 1969, or an average of about 3.2 million jobs destroyed each year. During this period approximately 110 jobs were created for every 100 jobs that were destroyed by plants shutting down. This ratio represents a sharp reduction in the job-creation capacity evidenced by the economy during the 1950s and 1960s. This stalled economic motor is further illustrated by the striking increase in the rate of unemployment during the decade. Between 1970 and 1981 the rate of unemployment soared from 5% to approximately 10%.

The various regions of the United States experienced this economic slowdown differentially. For instance, the northwestern corridor experienced a net loss of jobs. Alternatively, the sunbelt had the greatest net gain of jobs in the country (Bluestone and Harrison, 1982). The differential pattern of growth and decline has clearly contributed to the migratory pattern of workers from the northeast and midwest to the south, southwest, and far west in search of employment. These southern and western states, however, have been increasingly unable to absorb this surplus group of laborers into their workforce. This message did not reach the droves of dislocated workers who continued until recently to migrate south in the 1980s only to learn that jobs, housing, and social services are as in short supply in Houston, Texas, as they are in Cleveland, Ohio, or Buffalo, New York.

Underlying the inflation, job loss, unemployment, and migration of the 1970s is a crisis of capital accumulation. As Ian Gough (1979) has noted:

The combined G.N.P. of the O.E.C.D countries (Organization for Economic Cooperation & Development) between 1973 and 1975 fell by five percent, industrial output plummetted and world trade declined 14 percent . . . underlying the halt to accumulation on the world scale has been the decline in the motor force of capitalist economies: profits. In the U.S., West Germany . . . and the United Kingdom the last decade has witnessed a long-term decline in the profitability of industrial and commercial companies [Gough, 1979].

Such economic conditions remain in the 1980s.

In response to declining profits, specific labor-intensive industries such as autos and steel disinvested and redirected their capital investments elsewhere. Alternatively, emergent, highly profitable service or hi-tech industries, such as electronics, computers, and McDonald's have benefited from substantial investments. The hi-tech industries' profitability can in part be traced to this new technology's rapid introduction into a variety of workplaces. This process has helped reduce labor costs in particular industries. For instance, the insurance industry has used a combination of word processors and computers to both reduce its workforce and increase productivity (Working Women, 1980).

Just as important, the emergent new economy of hi-tech and service industries has a bipolar income distribution. Between 1973 and 1980, 70% of all new private-sector jobs created were low paying. Annual average salaries for these fields in 1980 were less than $12,500 (Rothschild, 1981). Rothschild underscored the recent job creation record of this sector of the economy when she noted that:

Food, health and business services produced more than 3 million jobs between 1973 and 1979. This sector of the economy generated more than 40 percent of the new private jobs created between 1973 and the summer of 1980. These three service industries' employment increased three times as fast as total private employment and sixteen times as fast as employment in the goods producing or industrial sectors of the economy.

The 1980s have seen an intensified development of that dual labor market. The hi-tech industries are generating some high-paying jobs. However, the bulk of new jobs being generated in hi-tech and service industries offer relatively modest wages. As Bluestone and Harrison (1982) have indicated, "the majority of jobs . . . are hardly sufficient to provide an adequate standard of living for the normal sized family." A family is required to take two full-time jobs at a McDonald's food outlet or in a discount department store. Most of the jobs being created in the fields of computers or electronics essentially duplicate McDonald's wage structure. At the same time that low-paying jobs are being rapidly created, relatively high-paying manufacturing jobs are being destroyed. Capital-investment decisions are removing these jobs, which paid an average annual salary of $22,000 (Bluestone and Harrison, 1982). Manufacturing jobs are being relocated from the unionized and high wage structures of the northeast and midwest to the nonunionized and relatively low wage structures of the south and Third World. Recent negotiations between the unions and manufacturers in each of these industries have resulted in substantial wage concessions in return for some modest job-security provisions.

Each of these trends has contributed to the depression of wages for most workers. Those displaced from mill, auto, or steel jobs must make a leap to high-wage/skill jobs or fall to lower-paying, unstable work. The middle-level jobs (as represented by the old manufacturing line-level work) are rapidly disappearing and the choices are therefore much starker for workers. Recent evidence suggest that for two reasons it is very difficult for displaced workers to make this transition. The skills necessary to fill high-level positions, for instance, in the fields of electronics or computers are substantial. The opportunities for a middle-aged father or a single mother to acquire these skills are minimal. In effect, the educational and financial supports necessary to enable substantial numbers of displaced workers to make this transition do not exist. Second, and just as important, the very structure of the new job market prohibits such movement. As has already been noted, the overwhelming majority of new jobs are low paying and unstable. A relatively small proportion of new jobs are at the upper end of this earnings pyramid. Consequently, at best, only a small fraction of displaced workers could be absorbed at the upper end of this wage continuum.

The restructuring of the economy as a result of the fiscal crises is contributing at least in the short run to a general reduction of wages. As has already been noted, unionized workers in manufacturing industries will gradually give back concessions on wages, pensions, and other benefits because of the capacity of capital to disinvest and move its jobs elsewhere. Alternatively, workers who are displaced will make the more rapid fall to either jobs that pay close to the minimum wage or to chronic unemployment. Finally, many of those entering the labor market will quickly learn that they cannot duplicate the peak earnings of their parents.

We think it important to repeat that the reduction of wages is part of a dynamic process. This same process unfolded in earlier historic periods of economic crisis. As E.P. Thompson noted,

> The first half of the 19th century must be seen as a period of chronic underemployment, in which the skilled trades are like islands threatened on every side by technological innovation and by the in rush of unskilled or juvenile labor . . . we must bear in mind the insecurity of many skills in a period of rapid technical innovation and of weak trade unions. . . . In a number of trades which Thomas Large noted as both organized and highly paid in 1812 there was a serious deterioration in the status and living conditions over the next 30 years [Thompson, 1963: 241, 243].

Declining living standards were also experienced by the unemployed during this period. It was in 1834 that the Doctrine of Less Eligibility was applied to the unemployed. This law mandated that relief grants be kept below the wages of the lowest-paid laborer (Piven and Cloward, 1972). Given the laws of the marketplace and the corollary Doctrine of Less Eligibility, the reduction of wages during this period required a comparable reduction in the size of relief grants. The substantial reductions in relief benefits between 1820 and 1840 placed many families below subsistence levels of income. This historic set of circumstances also has its contemporary parallels. The social wage recently available to chronically unemployed (A.F.D.C. mothers, G.A. recipients, the physically disabled and elderly) and dislocated workers (recently unemployed and hungry) through welfare-state benefits is being redefined by the present fiscal crisis and the consequent reduction in marketplace wages. The relationship between this redefinition of the social wage and the intensification of poverty will be developed in the next section of the chapter.

THE REDUCTION OF THE SOCIAL WAGE AND THE INTENSIFICATION OF POVERTY

Between 1930 and approximately 1975 the welfare state experienced an uninterrupted period of expansion. Benefits or entitlements to the aged, single mothers, unemployed workers, and the disabled expanded substantially. Just as significantly, increased groups of citizens were covered by various kinds of legislation and a range of entitlement services were developed. It is important to note that despite this expansion, welfare-state benefits did not address the basic employment, housing, and other survival needs of many low-income Americans. Additionally, there was much regional variation in the amount and kind of available benefits. For instance, benefits in New York and Massachusetts consistently have been far greater than entitlement levels in Mississippi or Arizona. Despite these qualifying statements, it is clear that the social wage or basement income that is assured all citizens through various entitlement programs increased substantially during this 50-year period. It is also apparent that increased numbers of citizens applied for and received these benefits. For instance, while the U.S. population between 1960 and 1970 increased 13%, the welfare population increased 94%, much of it concentrated in the older, larger central cities (there are 11.5 million recipients in the 10 largest cities) (Burghardt, 1983).

For the first time in American history, however, a mature welfare state is confronted with a fiscal crisis. The consequence has been an increased effort to redefine legitimating services or entitlements downward while concurrently redirecting welfare state resources to the private sector. These trends have intensified the difficult life circumstance of the poor.

THE REDUCTION OF THE SOCIAL WAGE

Recent reports by journalists, academics, advocates, and the government underscore the dramatic reduction of entitlement benefits and services. Between 1980 and 1984 there was an intensified drive to make across-the-board cuts in all social-welfare programs. As a result, funding for AFDC and child-welfare programs fell by 13% (Horowitz et al., 1984). Food stamps were cut 14% (Hopper and Hamberg, 1984). It is estimated that overall, cash welfare benefits declined by 17%. More specifically, these cuts eliminated one million people from food-stamp coverage. Additionally, 90% of the working families on AFDC had their benefits reduced or eliminated. Additionally, SSDI cuts affected 450,000 recipients (Rich, 1984). Finally, although general-assistance payments vary by locality, recent evidence indicates a substantial loss in the value of these benefits. It is important to note that these trends did not begin during Reagan's presidency but have been dramatically intensified by this administration.

These cuts have had a devastating impact upon many American citizens, as later chapters will spell out in detail. Newspapers and the visual media have dramatically illustrated the severe human costs associated with these cuts. It has been reported that 15.2% of all American citizens lived in poverty during 1983, the highest proportion since 1965. As recently as 1980, 13% of Americans fell below the poverty line (Joe and Rogers, 1985). The Office of Management and Budget (OMB) indicated that budget reductions had pushed 520,000 citizens, 320,000 of whom were children, below the poverty line between 1981 and 1983. The Urban Institute discovered that during this three-year period, the Reagan Administration policies accounted for approximately 50% of the expansion in poverty (Urban Institute, 1984).

Consequently, increased numbers of citizens throughout the country are gravitating to public transportation centers, libraries, and the modest number of available shelters because of insufficient housing and grant levels that cannot meet prevailing rents. Additionally, many citizens are unable to meet their daily nutritional requirements. Recent reports have begun to document the toll that this epidemic of hunger has taken on the health of a range of vulnerable groups. Just as important, substantial numbers of physically disabled people were forced to return home or to institutions when their Social Security Disability Insurance checks were halted between 1981 and 1983. In general, the elimination of this benefit dramatically disrupted many physically disabled citizens' capacity to live independently, and significantly reduced the quality of their lives. For other citizens living on fixed incomes, such as the elderly (Social Security) and poor female headed families (A.F.D.C.) recent budget cuts have heightened the stresses associated with daily life choices.

In effect, these citizens are increasingly forced to choose between eating and meeting the rent or paying the electricity as opposed to the heating bill. Media reports in the 1980s have also focused on the dead-end choices and deterioration of recently unemployed blue collar workers from the midwest. A number of studies have documented the increased alcoholism, child abuse, domestic violence, and despair that is associated with this unemployment. The tightening vise-like grip of this diminishing standard of living has intensified the daily struggles of the poor and in turn, dramatically increased stress levels for these most vulnerable groups of citizens.

What these data suggest is that the much discussed "safety net" is increasingly an illusion. When basic allowances are not sufficient to address fundamental needs, then clearly entitlement grants have more symbolic than real value. In effect, it is an entitlement that is increasingly incapable of meeting citizens' basic survival needs for permanent housing, food, and home care (disabled and elderly, and so on).

It is important to note that women and people of color have been disproportionately affected by these trends. Women, blacks, and Hispanics have incomes that are substantially less than the national median. It has been reported that when women are employed full time, they earn less than 60% of what men earn in full-time work (Urban Institute, 1984). Salary differentials are similar for black and Hispanic workers. Consequently, women, blacks, and Hispanics have had to rely on social-service programs (Coalition on Women and the Budget, 1984). This reliance has increased in recent years as the share of the U.S. population living below the poverty line has increased substantially. Census data suggests that between 1979 and 1982 the number of people living in poverty rose from 26.1 million to 34.4 million persons or from 11.7% to 15% of the population (Stallard et al., 1983). These trends are particularly telling for the black and Hispanic single mother.

> Among all women in families hurt by budget cuts, those who have the responsibility of providing the sole financial support for their families are the most vulnerable. For these families the spectre of poverty is an increasing reality. The percentage of families maintained by women increased from 10.7 percent . . . to 15.4 percent of all families. For Black families, the percentage of female maintained families is even greater, in 1983, 41.4 percent of Black families were maintained by women, an increase from 28 percent in 1970. In Hispanic families the percentage of female maintained families increased from 15 percent in 1970 to 23 percent in 1983 [U.S. Bureau of the Census, 1984; see also U.S. Bureau of Labor Statistics, 1984].

Clearly, the reduction of the social wage has had dramatic consequences for the poor. As has already been suggested, substantial cuts in entitlement allowances, and the disengagement of the federal government from the provision of discrete services is increasingly placing low-income people in the position of being unable to afford basic necessities. This combination of factors has in turn contributed to the rapid intensification of poverty for many citizens.

It is important to reiterate that each of these factors is in turn strongly associated with the fiscal crisis and changing structure of the job market. This combination of general wage reductions in the market place and social wage cuts flow out of dynamics within the marketplace. As Karl DeSchweinitz, E.P. Thompson, and others have suggested, this is a recurrent historic pattern during periods of fiscal crisis (Coalition on Women and the Budget, 1984).

Clearly, this is a period of economic resocialization. The labor force is being resocialized to expect new and lower wages. As has been suggested, in order to effect such reductions, the doctrine of less eligibility must be enforced. In effect, workers at the bottom of the labor force must understand that an even more reduced living standard awaits them outside the marketplace. Concurrent with marketplace wage reductions, entitlement levels are also being reduced. These reductions have both freed resources for alternative investments and substantially diminished the living standard of the nonworking poor.

Clearly, recipients of entitlements are also being resocialized. The Welfare Rights Movement of the 1960s and 1970s, which argued that all citizens have an economic right to an adequate standard of living, is being replaced by a public attitude that is rapidly recreating nineteenth-century definitions of entitlement. Increasingly, temporary shelters for the homeless are replacing housing, soup lines are being substituted for an adequate food allowance and reinstitutionalization is being emphasized at the expense of independent living. Once again, the state's social-service role is being reconstructed and translated into policies that reflect nineteenth-century approaches to poverty. It is no accident that present policies favor a reduced social-service role for the state.

CONCLUSION

During an earlier period of economic crisis, the 1930s, the social wage or base entitlement of workers was also recreated. In contrast to the erosion of benefits or economic rights of this period, the Great Depression witnessed an expansion of social-insurance programs and a gradual increase in the social wage. Advances in definitions of economic entitlement or the social wage continued, albeit gradually (as compared for instance to many western European countries), during the postwar economic boom. Many economists and historians have indicated that advances in the social wage during the 1930s was not a historic aberration or accident.

These improvements occurred precisely because various groups of workers and citizens organized and pressed their demands for economic benefits. Labor unions, the Townshend movement, Huey Long's followers, socialists and communists focused on the federal government or state as having a primary responsibility for assuring its citizens a certain minimum standard of living (Thompson, 1963; also see DeSchweinitz, 1975). This represented a marked shift, for in earlier historic periods the church and private agencies were expected to assume this social function. Between 1934 and 1936 this conflict peaked and various reforms were enacted that increased social-insurance benefits and coverage. In effect, the intensified class conflict of this period forced certain social-wage concessions. Simultaneously, the states' increased investment in social programs helped to preserve social harmony as militancy ebbed by the late '50s.

The expansion of many social entitlements during an approximate 50-year period strengthened the economic position of many citizens. The entitlements functioned to cushion many groups of workers from the instability of the marketplace. Unemployment insurance, disability benefits, AFDC, and other entitlements guaranteed those deemed eligible a minimum standard of living. During this period, however, many people were excluded from such benefits, for example, agricultural workers and women engaged in domestic labor.

Clearly, however, present trends are unraveling many of the advances of the last 50 years. For instance, shelters, soup lines, and institutions do not offer those who are presently homeless, hungry, or disabled a basis for recreating their lives. At best, most of these services temporarily halt the physical, emotional, and intellectual deterioration of those citizens who are falling below the "safety net." These services also reflect a more general diminution of the social wage. Clearly, if the needs of the homeless, chronically unemployed, or temporarily unemployed are to be met, then economic entitlements must be expanded or advanced, not diminished. If this pattern is to be halted, however, an alternative agenda must be developed.

In the next chapter we will examine how recent budget-cutting trends have affected the circumstance of the homeless, hungry, disabled, elderly, recently unemployed and poor female-headed families. Just as important, the mythologies associated with each of these groups of citizens that have contributed to the formation of past and present social policies, will be explored in each chapter. Finally, and perhaps most important, the new forms of practice that are emerging in response to these populations' intensified needs will be reviewed and discussed. More specifically, practice approaches that are organized to address both the immediate crises and long-term entitlement/service needs of each of these groups of citizens will be highlighted.

Chapter 2

HOMELESSNESS

John Bradford was aimlessly wandering around the street searching for housing. His family waited for him at the Half-Moon motel hoping he would miraculously rescue them before their resources evaporated. John, a worker at a produce market, was earning $12 an hour. The Bradford family had been paying $30 a day for their room at the Half-Moon motel since they were evicted from their apartment. The motel costs ate up so much of the family's weekly income that little money was left over for food, no less the security deposit to obtain an apartment. The Bradford family's daily worry was that they would soon wind up homeless on the streets. The family's break-up due to the intervention of state child-welfare agencies also seemed imminent.

In recent years the homeless person wandering aimlessly on the streets has become as strongly associated with the imagery and reality of American urban life as perhaps the skyscraper was approximately 25 years ago. Increasingly, we find large numbers of homeless citizens in train stations, bus terminals, and public parks. The public perception of the homeless is that they are almost without exception incoherent, disoriented, substance abusers, physically diseased, and ultimately without hope. This stereotypic profile is at odds with the reality. The ranks of the homeless are expanding every day with new citizens who are in most respects little different than the rest of us. Their plight is not a consequence of some genetic or individual defect, but rather a confluence of social forces that are driving a range of American citizens into the most abject poverty witnessed in this country since the "Great Depression."

WHO ARE THE HOMELESS?

Perhaps the first question that must be asked then about the homeless is: Who are they? Clearly, the first wave of homelessness in the late 1970s was dominated by psychiatric patients who were recently released from state mental hospitals. For instance, in New York State approximately 126,000 patients were released between 1965 and 1977 (Baxter and Hopper, 1981). States like California closed many of its largest mental hospitals between 1970 and 1972 (Flynn, 1985). The number of patients in U.S. mental hospitals dropped to 150,000 in 1978 from a peak of 650,000 in the mid 1950s (Leepson, 1982). At the same time this policy of deinstitutionalization was being implemented, however, few services were developed either to house or support former mental patients. These vulnerable populations then gravitated to single room occupancy hotels (S.R.O.s), which were the cheapest source of housing in urban areas. However, between 1970 and 1982 more than 110,000 S.R.O. units, representing 87% of the total supply, were lost in New York City. Nationally, approximately 1.2 million or 47% of the total supply of S.R.O.s disappeared (Baxter and Hopper, 1984). Additionally, the Reagan Administration cut off 700,000 of the 4.3 million people on the S.S.I. rolls. While the mentally disabled accounted for only 11% of the people on the rolls they experienced 31% of the cuts (Hope and Young, 1984). This combination of factors drove many ex-mental patients into the streets. Present estimates suggest that between 20% and 50% of most urban homeless populations comprises psychiatrically disabled individuals. For instance, recent data suggest that 34% of the shelter inhabitants in New York City were former mental patients (Crystal, 1984).

Another group of individuals generally associated with the phenomena of homelessness is substance abusers. Citizens with alcohol or drug problems had accounted, up to the late 1960s, for almost all of the known homeless in "flop houses," while drug addicted individuals were more frequently isolated and living in burnt-out or condemned buildings. Reverend John McVean of New York City's St. Francis of Assisi Church has noted that "when I came to New York in 1969 the homeless tended to be older alcoholics. But since the early 1970s the most dramatic increase has been in the numbers of released mental patients" (Leepson, 1982). Although the proportion of the homeless, whose primary destabilizing experience is substance abuse, has declined, the vulnerability of this population to homelessness has been exacerbated by recent budget cuts. The Federal Omnibus Act of 1981 slashed block grants for mental health, alcohol, and drug abuse by 25%.

Another factor that has recently contributed to an expansion of homelessness is unemployment. The series of recessions during the 1970s and early 1980s has had a particularly devastating impact upon young and middle-aged workers who were dependent upon declining industries such as autos and steel. These groups of citizens have disproportionately absorbed the burden of unemployment and have had a most difficult time entering or reentering the labor market. Recent estimates suggest that the ongoing unemployment rate for young minority people is upward of 80% in many urban areas (Gary, Indiana; San Jose, California; and so on). Additionally, young white working-class males are having a difficult if not impossible time breaking into the industries that often sustained their families for generations, that is, rubber, autos, and steel. Finally, many workers who have lost their jobs during this period are unable to locate employment that even approximates their earlier earning power.

The difficulty of obtaining work locally in combination with the already stressed circumstances of their nuclear families has caused many recently unemployed citizens to search elsewhere for a full-time job. Recent reports suggest that these job searches often end in futility and frustration. The tent cities emerging in urban areas throughout the southwest and the more frequent reports of families living out of their cars in National Parks is a constant reminder that homelessness is no longer exclusively primarily a consequence of mental instability or drug abuse. Other evidence has also emerged that links homelessness to unemployment.

The city of New York's Human Resources Administration has reported that 25% of the recent applicants to the men's shelters are there because of job loss (Stoner, 1984). It is important to note that this group represents a large and growing proportion of the homeless in the late 1970s and early 1980s (Salerno et al., 1984).

Perhaps the most rapidly expanding subpopulation of the homeless are A.F.D.C. recipients who can no longer afford prevailing urban rents. It has been suggested that A.F.D.C. payments are between 20% and 60% below prevailing urban rents. There are a number of clear and concrete consequences of the gap between housing benefits and rental costs. Cities such as New York, Chicago, Milwaukee, Denver, and others too numerous to cite have reported dramatic increases in eviction rates (Salerno et al., 1984). The majority of these actions have been taken against low-income citizens. For instance in New York City a half-million eviction actions were initiated out of a total stock of two million rental units. Approximately 50% of these proceedings involved citizens on public assistance (Hopper & Hamberg, 1984). The consequence has been that A.F.D.C. families are increasingly losing their housing and falling into a state of homelessness.

The exponential increase in the number of homeless A.F.D.C. families has been staggering. During an approximate six-year period the number of homeless families in New York City has increased from less than 500 to 3,200 (totaling about 11,000 individuals). Alternatively, the number of homeless individuals within the sheltering system is approximately 6,850. This rapid shift in the makeup of the homeless population was best described by Bob Hayes (President of the National Coalition to House the Homeless) when he recently remarked that over half of the individuals presently homeless in New York City are children. Similar changes in the makeup of the homeless population are also being reported in cities as diverse as Tulsa, Madison, Los Angeles, Detroit, and Houston (Salerno et al., 1984).

Homelessness can also be traced to domestic violence. Battered women who choose to leave their violent spouses are often rendered homeless. They find they are frequently unable to recreate their housing through friends or family. Consequently, battered women (and their children) are placed in the position of having to rely upon churches and public agencies for shelter. Between 1974 and 1982 approximately 300 shelters were created for battered women (Shecter, 1982). It has been suggested that the battered women's movement grew substantially during this period. Clearly, both the increased number of shelters and size of this movement suggest that there is a rapidly expanding pool of battered women who for both short and extended periods of time are effectively homeless.

Recent demographic data also underscore the heterogeneity of the homeless population. More than 50% of homeless individuals are male (Stoner, 1984). Among the unattached homeless (non-familial) over 50% are males under 49 (Stoner, 1984). Additionally, 40% are white and 44% are black. The remaining 12% are comprised of Hispanic, Asian, Native American, and other ethnic minorities (Stoner, 1984).

Clearly, the stereotypical perceptions of the homeless do not jibe with the reality. The homeless are not simply the bag ladies or alcoholics. Instead, they are comprised of a cross-section of Americans who despite their differences in age, former income, education, prior jobs, and entitlement benefits have fallen into a common state of homelessness. Just as important, the proportion of Americans who can be neatly described and often dismissed as homeless because of personal inadequacy (alcoholics and mentally disabled) is rapidly being eclipsed by those citizens who are homeless because of economic dislocation (unemployment, battered women, A.F.D.C. families).

It is also apparent that the total number of homeless people is rapidly expanding. One of the primary debates between homeless advocates and public-sector decision makers concerns the number of homeless locally and nationally. The different estimates of the number of homeless can in part be traced to the logistical difficulties associated with establishing a homeless count. How do you at any single point in time conduct a head count of the homeless in burnt-out buildings, bus terminals, or on the streets? Clearly, at best all one can establish is a "guesstimate." Advocates' numbers are relatively high because they need to dramatize the problem and thus pressure the public sector to act. Alternatively, the government has an interest in minimizing both the size of the problem and its resource allocation given the competing demands on its scarce dollars during a period of fiscal austerity.

It is within this context that recent estimates on the number of homeless nationally range between one and three million. More specifically, rough estimates have been developed for selected cities: 60,000 in New York City, 35,000 in Los Angeles, 25,000 in Chicago, 15,000 in Baltimore, 2,500 in Denver, 2,000 in Boston, 2,000-3,500 in Atlanta, 7,700 in St. Louis, 8,000 in Philadelphia, 10,000 in San Francisco, and 6,500 in Detroit (Baxter and Hopper, 1984). These numbers suggest homelessness is a national problem that is defining the life circumstance of an alarmingly high proportion of this country's population.

INADEQUATE RESPONSE TO THE PROBLEM

The primary service response to homelessness has been to develop temporary shelters. These shelters have generally been created through a combination of private and public money. Clearly, however, as in the 1930s, churches and other private institutions simply do not have the resources to meet even a small fraction of this sheltering need. However, the response of federal, state, and local units of government is woefully inadequate given the substantial and growing problem of homelessness. Illustrations abound of the shortfall between public-sector expenditures and need.

In December 1982, approximately 700-10,000 beds were available to the 20,000-25,000 homeless people in Chicago. About 100 of these beds were financed by the public sector. The private shelters were filled to capacity each night and regularly turned away between 30 and 50 people a day (Salerno et al., 1984). In Cleveland there were 370 beds for a homeless population that is conservatively estimated as ranging between two and three thousand. During the month of September 1982 Cleveland shelters were forced as a result of inadequate space to turn away 737 individuals (Salerno et al., 1984). Denver is a city with one of the best ratios of beds to homeless people. Its services, however, still fall far short of need; in January 1983 Denver had 682 shelter beds for a homeless population of about 2,500. Almost all of the beds are being provided by private church groups such as the Salvation Army, The Catholic Worker, and Samaritans. The inadequacy of the response is underscored by the fact that during a typical week in the winter of 1982-1983 the Samaritan shelter had to turn away 125 homeless individuals and 31 homeless families because they had no available beds or floor space. Additionally, St. Vincent's de Paul Shelter has had to turn away 35 homeless people every week because of insufficient space (Salerno et al., 1984).

The gap between shelter beds and the number of homeless is also acute in coastal urban areas such as Los Angeles and New York. There are about 2,400 beds for the approximately 35,000 homeless people in Los Angeles. The public perception has been that the problem of homelessness was effectively resolved in New York City by the courts. The Callahan v. Carey case litigated in 1979 by Bob Hayes resulted in the New York Supreme Court granting a preliminary injunction requiring the city to provide sufficient beds for those homeless men who applied for shelter. This landmark decision also required New York City to

> provide shelter (including clean bedding, wholesome board and adequate security) and supervision to any person who applies for shelter at the Men's Shelter [*Callahan v. Carey*].

It was argued that on the basis of state statutes, social service laws, and the city's administrative code, all homeless men have a right to food and shelter. The court's decision resulted in the immediate creation of 5,000 public-sector beds. Interestingly, the number of "public beds" in New York City has consistently outstripped the total available throughout the rest of the country. Despite this relatively substantial investment, in 1984 only 18,000 beds (individuals and families) were available for between 36,000 and 60,000 homeless people in New York City (Hayes, 1985). Once again, the need for emergency shelter is far greater than the available space or beds. Why then are some public-shelter beds constantly available except during the coldest period(s) of the winter?

The quality of life in most public shelters is so abysmal that many people choose to remain or return to the streets rather than live in these public facilities. The living space is often dirty, highly confined, and offers no privacy. Older, weaker, and more vulnerable homeless people are frequently preyed upon by workers and other residents. The price one may pay for residing in a shelter can be as small as being pushed to the back of the meal line or as large as being robbed of one's few remaining possessions and physically assaulted. These "warehouses" of the homeless have also been characterized as dimly lit, overcrowded, and understaffed. The combination then of fear, overcrowding, increased vulnerability to crime, and insufficient services have persuaded many homeless people to avoid public shelters unless their very survival is threatened on the streets. John R. Coleman, president of the Edna McConnel Clark Foundation, after spending 10 days on the streets of New York in the middle of winter, described the men's shelter in East New York.

> The lobby and the adjacent sitting room were jammed with men standing, sitting or stretching out in various positions on the floor. It was as lost a collection of souls as I could have imagined. Old and young, scarred and smooth, stinking and clean, crippled and hale, drunk and sober, ranting and still parts of another world and parts of this [Coleman, 1983].

It is important to understand that rejection of a shelter bed has serious implications for the homeless person. They are saying that bus stations, backstreets, and alleys where they are preyed upon by robbers known as "jackrollers" or in the case of women, vulnerable to emotional, sexual, or physical abuse is preferable to life in the shelters. Additionally, homeless people know only too well the physical and emotional consequences of living on the streets for extended periods of time.

Physical disease (malnutrition, tuberculosis, etc.), the severe emotional distress of constantly struggling to meet basic survival needs, being spurned by other poor and the middle class as a leper with whom one risks infection by even making eye contact, and the constant search for warmth and sustenance are as basic to the nightmarish life on the streets as daydreaming is to a school child. Think then about just how abhorrent the conditions must be in many public shelters if homeless people choose to embrace the powerlessness, despair, and physical dangers of the street. This choice is perhaps the most powerful indictment of public shelters as they are presently organized.

A supplemental service (to shelters) potentially available to homeless people is emergency assistance. Many states (New York, Massachusetts, New Jersey, etc.) have statutes or codes that require municipalities to provide time-limited assistance to individuals or families who are homeless. These statutes can be invoked to require the locality (if there are insufficient shelter beds) to sustain homeless people in alternative settings, for instance, motels. One of the most effective attempts to enforce emergency assistance statutes through advocacy services has occurred in Elizabeth, New Jersey.

Prior to this advocacy project, it was discovered that the city of Elizabeth resisted every effort by homeless people to secure emergency assistance. Without exception each of the requests made independently by homeless people to municipal welfare was denied. The applicants had been provided with one of several standard responses to their initial request for assistance. Some homeless people were advised, for example, to first obtain an address or residence in the city of Elizabeth and return later in the day. In certain instances, applicants unable to furnish proof of any residence in Elizabeth were advised to return to their previous residence. A number of clients were simply provided transportation money for the purpose of seeking shelter or obtaining assistance in neighboring communities. Other homeless citizens arriving at the welfare office late in the morning (e.g., 10:30 or 11:00 A.M.) had been informed that it was too late to receive benefits and were instructed to return the next day (Fabricant and Epstein, 1984).

Clearly, stringent eligibility requirements and the seeming inaccessibility of income-support programs critically hampers the homeless person's capacity to stabilize his or her life circumstance. The difficulty of gaining access to income supports is also illustrated by the New York City Project Reach Out's experience with S.S.I. Between 1981 and 1982 this program was unable to establish the eligibility of any of its clientele of recently released psychiatric patients for S.S.I. All of their clients were turned down regardless of the severity of their disability (Baxter and Hopper, 1984).

Finally, it must be noted that the primary policy responses to homelessness are fundamentally flawed because they have maintained an almost exclusive reliance upon brief time-limited residence (shelters) or assistance. The homeless person's basic need for permanent housing is effectively ignored by present policies and services. For instance, the $133 a month available through New Jersey's general and emergency assistance programs cannot begin to meet minimum rental costs and therefore assures the continued instability of recent applicants.

There are few, if any, services available to support the homeless persons' search for housing, effort to secure an entitlement (advocacy), or attempt to stabilize emotionally (counseling). Such services are critical if the homeless person is to move from the streets or sheltering system to a more stable circumstance. The next section of this chapter will present a continuum of services capable of addressing both the crises of the homeless person's circumstance and stabilizing his or her life. Model service programs and practice approaches that are being developed throughout the country will be concretely incorporated into this discussion.

NEW PROGRAM AND PRACTICE APPROACHES

As has already been suggested, there are a continuum of concrete services that must be made available to homeless people. To begin with, service personnel must systematically and consciously reach out in the community to make contact with the homeless. Second, the constellation of services available to the homeless must address their immediate crises or emergency assistance needs, i.e., food, shelter, advocacy. Finally, and perhaps most important, stabilization services must provide a basis for permanent housing, jobs, etc. The potential mix of approaches within each of these service categories will be specifically addressed in the following discussion.

CONTACT SERVICES

For a variety of reasons these frontline efforts are often most critical in establishing a rapport with homeless people and a basis for the *future* development of pertinent services. After an extended period of time on the street, many homeless people may not be able to utilize effectively particular services because they are severely disorganized, disoriented, or suffering from a combination of physical disabilities. The homeless person may choose to ignore social-service programs because their experience with agencies has been less than satisfactory. For instance, mentally disabled homeless people may have had particularly painful experiences in mental hospitals. Additionally, young people who are recently unemployed or unable to secure an initial job may have had different but similarly disturbing experiences with foster parents and child welfare institutions.

These groups of citizens then may have to be encountered by service workers with particular sensitivity and on numerous occasions before they are persuaded to avail themselves of formal services. It is the contact or outreach worker's responsibility to engage this understandably fearful, resistant, and perhaps frustrated population. Contact workers must provide the homeless with the substantive information necessary to link them with the critical emergency assistance or stabilization services potentially available in the community. Quite clearly, before this information can be effectively conveyed, the homeless person must be sufficiently engaged to trust the service worker. Therefore the outreach person must work in a relaxed and informal manner.

The availability of services cannot be discussed until the homeless person is able to consider the possibility of reentering the formal agency system. This process therefore requires that contact workers engage in an "open-ended" process of attempting to establish working relationships with homeless people throughout the community. Relatedly, such work demands numerous contacts over an extended period of time with homeless people. Such efforts will therefore require patience, an independent interest in establishing relationships with homeless people, and a constantly updated inventory of services available in the community.

Additionally, contact services can perform the independent function of providing services to homeless people wherever they may reside. Food, medical kits, health services, and so on, can be made available to homeless people in bus terminals, train stations, burned-out buildings, and on the streets. These services are intended to sustain, momentarily, homeless people by addressing on a very temporary and ad hoc basis their malnutrition and physical illnesses.

Outreach efforts must also be organized to collect pertinent data about homeless people in the community. For instance, a permanent record should be kept of the age, gender, familial structure, and other characteristics of the homeless. Additionally, the physical condition of the homeless person, his or her recent experience with entitlement services, and efforts to locate housing should also be documented. Finally, these contact services (particularly in smaller communities) should enable service personnel to begin projecting the total number of homeless people in the locality.

Such information is critical to (1) countering current mythologies or misconceptions concerning the homeless, (2) developing a service plan that addresses the magnitude and heterogeneity of need, and (3) creating the data base for future advocacy or litigation on behalf of the homeless. For instance (regarding point two), outreach efforts have consistently indicated that people remaining on the streets are more elderly and disabled than the residents of shelters. This population may feel that their relative vulnerability is greater in the shelters than the streets. If this is the case, then new sheltering services need to be created that address the particular needs of the frail elderly and mentally disabled homeless.

A range of specific outreach programs have been created during the past five years. For instance, Angel's Flight in Los Angeles and Children of the Night in Hollywood represent attempts to make contact with runaway youths, at bus depots and on the streets before pimps can reach them. Another program, Project Reach Out in New York, has attempted to make contact with the growing number of street people on the upper West side of Manhattan. These outreach teams sometimes briefly encounter the homeless by offering a cup of coffee, a sandwich, or conversation. At other times more intensive efforts are made to meet the physical or emotional needs of the person. Other outreach programs in New York City include Midtown Outreach and Project Help.

The makeup of outreach teams usually evolves over time as in the case of Project Reach Out, which began with a generalist M.S.W. and paraprofessionals but over time recruited more and more workers with particular expertise or specialization(s). For instance, it was determined during the course of the outreach efforts that particular services were needed in the areas of mental health, alcoholism, drug abuse, and income maintenance. Increasingly, staff are also multilingual because of the needs of immigrants and other non-English-speaking clients. Other outreach programs for the homeless exist in Boston, San Francisco, and Chicago.

After these outreach efforts, an attempt is sometimes made to bring people in off the streets and place them in voluntary drop-in centers. For instance, the Anthony Oliveri Center in New York City serves approximately 105 homeless women a day who are fearful of the public shelters. This kind of center and similar settings in Los Angeles (Downtown Womens Center) and Philadelphia (Arch Street Drop-In Center) encounter a segment of the homeless who would otherwise remain distanced or isolated from the service system. These settings are generally tolerant and accepting. They require no intake forms and do not try to change people. Consequently, these services are utilized extensively by otherwise resistant and frightened homeless people.

These centers generally provide the following services: delousing, a place to sleep, a meal, and advocacy. Usually, the Drop-In Center is so overcrowded that people have to sleep on mats or chairs. Clearly their appeal is access and informality for those homeless who are frightened of public institutions. It has been suggested that "characteristically, the staff of many of these programs are both caring and sensitive; they do not counsel or preach, make few demands and encourage self help and peer support" (Shifren-Levine, 1984).

Ideally, a case management function should be built into the provision of services for homeless people at the earliest stages of contact. The case manager should have ongoing oversight responsibility for a caseload of homeless people and ensure the availability, adequacy, and security of services for each of their clients. These "generic" social workers would provide brokerage services (to link clients with appropriate services), advocacy (to assure the provision of services from often recalcitrant or overworked agencies), community work (to develop or locate formal and informal services), clinical skills (diagnostic and therapeutic), and rehabilitation (which may mean a primary emphasis on locating housing or attempting to achieve very small simple changes in the clients' basic living skills) (Fabricant, 1983).

A question that is often raised about this package of services is whether any single worker can possess all of these skills. It is clear however, for all of the reasons cited in this chapter, such a combination of general skills are critical if the worker is to begin even addressing the multiple and acute problems of the homeless person. A number of programs are attempting to provide some case-management services at the point of contact with the homeless person. It should be noted that to our knowledge no program retains oversight case-management functions as homeless people move from contact to emergency assistance to stabilization services. In part, this is a consequence of workers at every stage of this continuum being so overloaded with the magnitude and complexity of the problems with which they are presently confronted that they can do little more than respond to the immediate crises.

Their capacity for follow-up services if the individual moves on to emergency assistance or stabilization services is almost nonexistent. Clearly, the limitations that plague the case manager can also haunt the outreach worker who gains the trust of a homeless person but is unable to broker an appropriate referral because the necessary services do not exist or are filled to capacity. It is important to reiterate that this section of the chapter is intended to present the mix of services that homeless people require and to identify specific programs that address these needs. However, present efforts are at best very limited because they can only address a small fraction of the need.

The resources that are necessary to address the client contact seriously, emergency assistance and stabilization needs of all homeless people, are presently unavailable. This reality critically affects the practice of even the most effective programs and able workers. We will return to this question of resource limitation(s) in the last section of the chapter.

The present discussion, however, will continue to focus on the types of programs and practice approaches that have made a positive difference in the lives of homeless people. We believe it is important to first establish that many of the critical needs of homeless people are being addressed through program and practice approaches that have been implemented. Only in this way can the present practice and policy dialogue on homelessness shift from an almost exclusive preoccupation with technical problem solving (what programs or practice modalities are most effective) to the at least equally compelling need of determining how to affect a substantially increased allocation of resources.

EMERGENCY ASSISTANCE: SHELTERS AND ADVOCACY

The second step in the provision of services to the homeless is specifically concerned with sheltering and advocacy. As has already been noted most shelters have a number of characteristic problems that account for the marginal existence it offers homeless people and relatedly its propensity to drive people back to the streets. Any discussion of shelters must therefore begin with a description of the qualities such a setting must possess if it is both to attract the homeless and improve their circumstance.

In general, the shelters that have been found to be most effective have low staff-to-resident ratios and have no more than 100 residents. Once a residence exceeds these limits, it often takes on the characteristics of total institutions. The large barrack shelters offer no privacy, few services, rigid bureaucratic procedures, and little, if any, security. For instance, the standard operating procedure of all large shelters (and many of the smaller residences) is that residents must vacate the facility right after breakfast and cannot return until late afternoon. Additionally, no bed commitments are made to homeless people. Consequently, many people may return in the evening only to find that their space has been given to someone else. These facilities generally distribute beds on a first-come first-served basis.

In part, this is a consequence of the scarcity of shelter space relative to demand. Just as important, it reinforces, in a rather arbitrary way, the temporal nature of shelter space and services. Clearly, such policies undermine the capacity of shelter staff to meet effectively the short- or long-term needs of their clientele. Instead, such shelters at best provide a dead-end service: beds on a rotating basis. The "revolving-door" quality of such shelters also affects the quality and content of support services. Rarely are staff available to provide necessary mental health or rehabilitation services on site. Entitlement-advocacy services are also rarely initiated. Finally, the critical need to engage in permanent-housing searches is all but ignored. This confluence of factors—insufficient beds, scarcity of staff, overcrowded residences, and poor living conditions—combine to define most public shelters in New York, Los Angeles, Chicago, and other urban areas as offering little more than the most basic elements of survival.

Temporary shelters, however, are capable of creating an environment of hospitality and developing support services that are both attractive and enabling. Shelters like Columbus House in New Haven, Connecticut "permit guests to reserve rooms for successive nights." Other shelters like Apostle House in Newark and Community Help in Park Slope (C.H.I.P.) in Brooklyn are specifically organized (through the type of staff that have been hired and the structure of the residence) to listen, provide comfort, and assist when asked. The Pine Street Inn (Boston) works to link its homeless residents with substance-abuse programs, psychiatric facilities, nursing homes, social security, welfare offices, housing, and work opportunities. Additionally, counseling services are provided on site.

A number of common threads unite these "alternative shelters." They share a fundamental regard for the dignity and human potential of their residents. This perspective has helped shape encounters between staff and residents that have been described as warm, caring, and cooperative. The consequent relationships have enabled staff to plan more effectively for and meet some of the needs of residents.

This philosophical underpinning and the concomitant structures that have evolved are further reinforced by these shelters' relatively low client-to-staff ratios. The relative availability of staff and volunteers enable the shelter to engage in the counseling, advocacy, and follow-up services that are critical to the permanent stabilization of homeless people. The emphasis on referral work "is rooted in the feeling that shelters are not a proper home for anyone" (Shifren-Levine, 1984). Finally, some of the shelters are prepared to sustain indefinitely those residents who are engaged in a prolonged search for an alternate placement.

Another type of emergency-assistance service is independent community-based advocacy. Such programs are expected to provide the case advocacy services necessary to assure that homeless people gain entry to discrete services (alcohol, drug, job programs) and entitlements. If the homeless are blocked from these services "class-advocacy approaches" can be utilized to force agencies or the government to address these unmet needs. Currently, the most popular form of class advocacy being utilized in behalf of the homeless is litigation. Various cases have been brought before the court, which include but are not limited to right to shelter, emergency-assistance provisions, and food allowances. Many of these cases were initially handled by advocates attempting to secure emergency assistance from local and county welfare systems. Other types of class-advocacy approaches, including political organizing (lobbying for legislation, rallies, etc.) are being employed in behalf of the homeless.

An organization that has been particularly effective in employing such advocacy tactics is the National Coalition to House the Homeless. In general, its approach has been to contest through the courts decision making of localities and social agencies that deny basic services to the homeless. The landmark decision Callahan v. Carey (which granted all homeless men in New York City a right to shelter) is perhaps the most significant legal victory to date of the coalition. In localities such as Los Angeles, coalitions have also been organized to litigate a range of issues specific to the circumstance of the homeless.

More multifaceted local-advocacy efforts have also emerged during the past decade. For instance, the Elizabeth (New Jersey) Coalition to House the Homeless has been engaged on an ongoing basis with advocacy work that simultaneously addresses the specific needs of individuals (cases) and the more general needs of the homeless as a class of citizens. The work of the Elizabeth coalition has contributed to (1) the provision of immediate emergency assistance by the locality to homeless people; (2) litigation that challenges present constraints on the provision of social services to the homeless; (3) the creation of nonprofit groups that are principally interested in developing more low-income housing; and (4) the emergence of a statewide coalition to pursue aggressively each citizen's right to housing. It has been suggested that the Elizabeth coalition's work is a model for advocacy services at a local and regional level.

STABILIZATION

Following a brief or extended stay in emergency shelter, permanent housing and support services must be secured for the homeless person. Too often, shelters are viewed as a final solution to the homeless person's problem. Clearly, homeless people value the permanence, privacy, and stability of housing no less than the rest of the population. The ultimate objective of every encounter with a homeless person must be to locate, depending upon need, independent or supportive living housing.

As has already been noted, one type of stabilizing service is supportive living. Generally, such housing has been made available to individuals recently released from mental hospitals. A model program of this type is Community Access on the lower east side of Manhattan. The program provides quality housing (safe and decent) to mentally disabled persons who might otherwise wind up in S.R.O.s (single-room occupancy), flop houses, or barracks-like shelters.

The clients of Community Access meet with their counselors at least three times a week and must be willing to work toward independent living. The social workers at Community Access perform case-management type functions. In effect, they work with residents to achieve short- and long-term goals. Additionally, advocacy services are offered to extend and protect the client's entitlement rights.

The residents of this program are generally "paired up" in apartment buildings. The program maintains 24-hour emergency coverage through a paging system. Programs of this kind, however, are very scarce. Community Access has estimated that another 5,000 citizens in New York City alone could utilize the range of services available through the program.

Another type of stabilizing service is residential communities that have been established by sectarian groups. An example of this type of service is the Franciscan residence in New York City. The general goal of the program is to help provide a humane and dignified life for its residents. Currently, 75 men and 25 women reside in this center. Again, space is scarce; in general an available apartment usually indicates that a tenant has died.

The rentals for these rooms range between $35 and $50 a week. Additionally, meals are provided for between 25 and 50 cents a day. Other services provided by the residence include the provision of (1) linkages with vocational and rehabilitation services, (2) advocacy to secure entitlements, and (3) money management. Unlike other residential settings the clientele does have access to staff and rarely has to wait in line for services. Additionally, on-site services are provided by Bellevue Hospital (psychiatric and medical twice a week), and the Human Resources Administration of New York City (crisis intervention).

It is important to note that this residence is also particularly committed toward building a tolerant community. These community features emphasize flexibility, patience, and respect in working with the mentally disabled and others. The following statement from the program's brochure describes the unusual qualities of this environment:

> The residents visit one another in hospitals, shop for or bring food to those who are ill and inform staff of the absence or problems of others. A high degree of unusual behavior and/or tolerance is tolerated. Second, third and fourth chances are given to those who are having difficulty. Birthdays are remembered and celebrated. To people with years of their lives spent behind mental hospital walls or on the streets, such decency is well-deserved and met with excitement and gratitude [Shifren-Levine, 1984].

Another type of stabilization service is independent housing that has service components, which emphasize job training and development. A prototype of the kind of stabilization service that is appropriate to the needs of the many homeless who are capable of living independently but require a job and housing to recreate their lives is Project Jericho in Manhattan. Since it was launched in 1983, the program has provided permanent housing for 100 formerly homeless adult men and women. Additionally, it has enabled many participants to return to the labor force. Program members may begin by working in Project Jericho's office, errand service, or house-cleaning service.

Perhaps, the most exciting program element of Project Jericho is its not-for-profit construction company. The company addresses the multiple needs of the homeless through a single program. In effect, homeless people are trained to build and renovate housing. Just as important, this new housing is set aside for the needs of the homeless. The combination of housing and job creation under the umbrella of this single program is one of the most novel and important programs that has been created during the past five years.

Additionally, Project Jericho is a community.

> People living together and doing things together. Every Friday night, we have a community meeting where there are speakers, entertainment or discussions. Sometimes quality of life issues such as how to handle money, health, etc. are discussed. Jericho also has a play troupe, arts and crafts group and chorale [Project Jericho brochure, 1984].

Entry to the facility is rather straightforward. The potential member is interviewed and expected to make his presence known "over the course of the following weeks by attending Friday night community meetings, doing volunteer work and joining evening activities" (Project Jericho brochure). Once the person is admitted and provided with a room appropriate support services are available. For instance, Project Jericho links its residents with drug abuse, alcoholism, and counseling services.

PRACTICE TENSIONS

Contact, emergency assistance, and stabilization work with the homeless will, by definition, produce a number of practice tensions. As has been noted on a number of occasions the services in the community necessary to meet the needs of all homeless citizens simply do not exist. The gap between the demand for and supply of contact, emergency, and stabilizing services is quite substantial. The specific dimensions of this shortfall have been noted in earlier sections of this chapter. It is currently sufficient to note that when a worker is attempting to develop an appropriate service plan and quickly learns that necessary referral services are nonexistent or unavailable, it is most frustrating.

Additionally, the fragmented nature of the social-service system also functions to limit the accessibility of needed services to homeless people. For instance, in New York City mentally ill drug abusers or alcoholics are generally unable to gain access to residential programs. In effect, the drug-abuse program defines the individual as mentally ill and the mental-health programs define the same person as a drug abuser. This definitional impasse leaves the homeless person with little hope for support services. This problem is particularly critical for homeless people because after an extended period of time on the street and in a downward spiral, they are struggling with multiple problems. In effect their circumstance is not reflected in the neat and, in this instance, artificial treatment categories of state and local programs. Again, the dissonance between the needs of homeless people and the procedures of state bureaucracies is a source of stress for service workers.

Additionally, the demands placed upon individual workers in settings that are generally understaffed and serving a particularly needy population can at times be overwhelming. The need to distance oneself from the constant and critical needs of the homeless is both appropriate and necessary. The essential issue for the service worker is how to distance oneself from this population. For instance, if the worker "withdraws" from the homeless by mocking their behavior, stereotyping their problems, or effectively rejecting their humanity, then at best only mechanical and ineffectual services can be delivered.

Distancing mechanisms must be established that insulate the worker from absorbing some of the pain, frustration, and demands associated with this type of practice. This effort is necessary if the worker is to retain a basic respect for homeless people, an interest in responding to identified need, and an enthusiasm for such work. Only in this way can the delicate balance necessary to sustain the worker and assure the provision of quality services be achieved. Certain variables that are prerequisites for achieving this balance include (1) the availability of private work space; (2) a capacity (at times) to separate emotionally from the problems of the client; (3)

co-worker supports and (4) an appreciation of the strengths and potential of homeless people.

Concomitantly, providers must develop a practice approach that avoids blaming the client for his or her circumstance. The pull toward "blaming the victim" is immense because the service worker is often confronted with the "individual symptoms" associated with homelessness (substance abuse, mental disability, and so on). The more hidden realities of housing shortages and grant levels that increasingly cannot buy entitlement recipients into the urban rental markets are more easily lost in this environment of personal crisis. It is critical, however, that workers force themselves to discover and rediscover that community pressures (housing scarcity and low grant levels) are primarily responsible for the explosion of individual and familial cases of homelessness.

Too often workers avoid looking at the dynamics of the housing market. It is critical that workers engage in housing searches so that they are consistently confronted with the social realities with which their clients must struggle daily. The substandard apartment that violates health and safety codes is at times available to the homeless person. The availability of such an apartment often places A.F.D.C. mothers in the position of having to choose between remaining in a shelter or moving to a new residence that is a potential or real threat to the family (rats, defective physical structure, and the like). Additionally, the homeless are frequently confronted in their housing searches with racism, prejudices against renting to families with children, and biases against welfare clients.

Each of these obstacles presupposes that housing exists at a price that the homeless can afford. As had already been noted, however, the primary obstacle that defeats the homeless during their forays into the housing market is the general unavailability of modestly priced apartments. These "social forces" consistently manifest themselves in the personal and familial struggles of the homeless. The stresses associated with racism, too little income, and life choices that offer little if any hope of alleviating suffering will over time wear people down and often result in the individual symptoms associated with homelessness, i.e., substance abuse, emotional disability, etc. Effective individual practice with the homeless requires that social-service workers look beyond individual symptoms, which too often lead to victim blaming, and alternatively explore the personal and social contexts that contribute to this breakdown.

CREATING SURVIVAL SERVICES

The circumstance of the homeless, however, cannot be fundamentally altered until the support services and housing that they require are created. In effect, the housing crisis and unavailability of services continue to combine to exacerbate the problems of the currently homeless and further destabilize the circumstance of the near homeless. As has been noted throughout this chapter, the vast majority of homeless cannot gain access to outreach, emergency-assistance, and stabilization programs because such services receive very modest funding relative to the magnitude of need. Even those homeless who graduate from these programs must often engage in extended housing searches and receive the necessary support services, and still cannot locate an apartment. Clearly, the housing and support services capable of making a dramatic difference in the lives of the homeless are woefully underfunded (given demand) or nonexistent. Consequently, the agenda for the 1980s and 1990s regarding the homeless must emphasize the creation of sufficient services and housing to meet present and future need.

In order to expand the pool of services and housing available to the homeless, pressure must be placed upon local, state, and federal governments. This can be accomplished by advocacy groups and service workers. They must attempt to heighten the visibility of the unmet needs of the homeless. Some of the tactics that are available to advocacy groups and service workers include litigation, rallies, lobbying with legislators, picketing public officials who are denying the homeless needed services, squatting in abandoned buildings, or engaging in civil disobedience at welfare centers.

A number of organizations are currently engaged in advocacy efforts that are intended to expand the services and housing available to the homeless. The National Coalition to House the Homeless has been involved in litigation to assure the availability of quality sheltering services. New Jersey Right to Housing has had homeless people speak about their circumstance at rallies, lobbying efforts and conferences. Other groups such as A.C.O.R.N. have squatted in abandoned buildings with homeless people. This tactic has dramatically identified a substantial block of housing (abandoned but salvageable buildings) which is available in every city to begin meeting the needs of the homeless. Just as important, this tactic announces that buildings defined as uninhabitable by the locality are often a better option than life on the streets.

The common thread that runs through these class-advocacy approaches is their singular understanding that exponential increases
in housing, quality shelters, and support services will have to occur
before the needs of the homeless can be met. Additionally, during
this period of fiscal crisis the public sector is unlikely to "volunteer" the resources or commitment necessary to stem the tide of
homelessness. Consequently, various forms of pressure will have
to be consistently applied before the fundamental dilemmas of the
homeless can be resolved. Many of the frustrations and tensions
experienced by service workers in shelters, outreach programs,
and stabilization services can be traced to the inadequate public
response to the problem of homelessness. It is in the interests of the
worker to contribute to activities that are potentially capable of
transforming the fiscal base and package of services available to
the homeless.

Only if workers make the vital connection between their often
equally untenable practice choices and a social environment that
limits options can redistributive efforts intended to benefit the
homeless have any chance of success. This realization, however,
must be followed by active forms of support for advocacy efforts
that are intended to advance the economic rights of the homeless.
In effect, class advocacy must be incorporated whenever possible
into the practice of line workers who are daily struggling with the
individual consequences of the most compelling and devastating
unmet need in our society. Clearly, only this approach offers a
basis for moving from stop-gap measures, which often cannot
address the most basic needs of the homeless, to long-term housing
and service solutions, which are capable of addressing the multiple
problems of this group of citizens.

APPENDIX 1:
Interventions with the Homeless

There is a range of interventions that need to be learned and
applied by practitioners interested in working with the homeless.
The interventions that will be discussed are often applied sequen-
tially. Clearly, the most immediate needs of the homeless are for
concrete survival services such as shelter. Therefore, the first type
of service often delivered to the homeless are advocacy services.
Advocacy services are specifically intended to enable the homeless
to obtain available services to meet their needs. The advocate must

have a knowledge of both available public and private services that can potentially meet the homeless person's need and the more specific circumstance of the individual or family with whom she or he is working. A number of concrete activities associated with homeless advocacy work include

(1) Obtaining background information on homeless people so that services can be matched with a range of needs (i.e., alcoholism, drugs, employment);
(2) "Walking" homeless individuals and families through local and county welfare so that they can receive their emergency-assistance entitlement;
(3) Working with church or other private groups to develop services to meet need;
(4) Assuring that the homeless are treated with dignity and respect once services have been arranged. Part of the advocate's responsibility therefore is to monitor private agencies.

Another intervention that needs to be developed for the homeless are support groups. These groups can be organized about the particular population characteristics (family, individual, women, men, etc.) or problem area (jobs, drugs, survival on the streets) of the homeless person. The group is intended to enable the homeless to connect with others who share similar problems and to work together to address or resolve these problems. The worker's function is to both facilitate these discussions and enable individuals to use these sessions as a problem-solving tool. Foci for such discussions might include

(1) the pooling of information and resources on available housing, etc.;
(2) how homeless individuals or families can pool their meager entitlement resources and expand their housing options;
(3) the particular problems of homeless women and children;
(4) identifying the personal and communal obstacles that undermine the homeless person's struggle to locate housing.

Another approach that must be used is class advocacy specifically intended to organize homeless people and others concerned about the problem of homelessness into a political force. This effort is intended to create pressure for expending additional resources and developing particular services to meet the needs of the homeless. Activities under the heading of class advocacy might include:

(1) the collection of information in the process of individual advocacy that might provide a basis for various types of advocacy;

(2) the homeless and their advocates testifying at legislative hearings about the paucity or inappropriateness of services;

(3) developing more dramatic or militant actions to dramatize the insufficiency of services. Such activities might include tent cities in front of city hall (in the absence of available suitable shelter space), referring people to the Mayor's house, etc.;

(4) squatting in abandoned buildings;

(5) intensifying intercity or interstate tensions by referring people to neighboring municipalities or states to dramatize a lack of services.

APPENDIX 2:
Skills Development

(1a) Review an incident that reveals your discomfort in working with the very poor or homeless. Identify the specific source of your discomfort (behavior, physical appearance, odor, fear, and so on).

(1b) How did you address or resolve these issues? Were you satisfied with this outcome? Have your practice choices strengthened or weakened your rapport with the homeless? Were other approaches available with which you felt less comfortable? If so, why? Identify these approaches and examine their potential effectiveness.

(2) How easily do you work in group situations? Do you feel a need to control the flow and direction of the discussion or do you have trouble defining your role and therefore become passive? What are your aspirations as a group leader or facilitator? Identify obstacles which might undermine, or have undermined, your aspirations. What other choices and/or roles are available to you that might enable you to work more effectively with the group? What supports, resources, etc., do you need to recreate your relationship to the group and thereby become a more effective practitioner?

(3) How can you use daily practice tasks, events, etc., to begin working with others (homeless, providers, citizens, etc.) to pressure for, and create, additional resources for the homeless? does such work pose any special problems? If so, identify and resolve. What problem areas, groups, etc., can provide a focus for your organizing in the short and long term? On what basis did you make such choices? (Availability of time, resources, immediate potential for alliances, interests of the group, etc.)

APPENDIX 3:
Check List

Do you feel sufficiently informed in the following critical areas of homelessness practice?

	Yes	No
(1) Are you familiar with a homeless person's range of potential entitlements under the following categories of assistance: (a) local assistance, (b) emergency assistance, (c) AFDC, (d) Social Security, (e) SSI and disability, (f) food stamps?	_____	_____
(2) Are you familiar with the type of information a homeless individual or family must make available to entitlement officials before they can become eligible for assistance?	_____	_____
(3) Do you know what shelter(s) or low-income housing is available in your community for the homeless?	_____	_____
(4) Do you know which agencies (private and public) are presently working with the homeless in your community?	_____	_____
(5) Do you know what resources are available in your community for shelter or housing creation?	_____	_____
(6) Can you identify private or public groups that are interested in expanding the options available to homeless people?	_____	_____

Chapter 3

THE HUNGRY

The winter temperature stood at 17 °F and the food line inside the store was long and only a bit disorderly as people lurched forward for the special item on display: Beluga caviar at "only" $29.50 an ounce. Zabar's, New York's most fashionable food emporium, was doing land-office business on its specially priced Russian delicacy. Outside the west side shop a hearty group of food-pantry volunteers from a local church were receiving a shorter but still steady stream of Zabar's shoppers who dropped in a little of their largesse: bagels, some cream cheese, a huge jar of pickles, loaves of French peasant bread. No one donated their caviar.

The donations were not surprising: They resembled an upscale version of what the hungry in America eat when forced to ration their food: starches that fill the stomach without providing nourishment. This little urban scene, repeated in shopping centers, malls, and streets across the United States gives a glimmer of the contradiction embedded in American life regarding food: Amidst the tremendous economic expanse that allows some daily gourmet specials, there are now more hungry people in America than at any time since the 1930s.

But how much hunger is there? There certainly isn't the famine and starvation found in countries like Ethiopia and Bangladesh. Is it an occasional missed meal or serious malnutrition? And whose responsibility is it to provide for those in need?

Hunger is in many ways an extremely difficult problem to assess. Unlike, say, Ethiopia, the problem is neither so severe nor so geographically constricted to one area of the country. (Nor, it must be said, so directly integral to the politics of the government.) Such devastation would focus the problem in more immediate terms that, fortunately yet ironically, is not possible here. In the United States it occurs among different people at different times of the month: for the welfare mother and her children, most often at the end of the month before her check arrives in the mail; for newly unemployed auto-workers it may happen when they arrive in a new region of the country and find there are neither jobs nor easy qualification for unemployment insurance; for the elderly senior, hunger may be a daily event because he or she is too proud for Supplemental Security Income (SSI). Joseph Lelyveld (1985), writing for the *New York Times* on hunger, described the "cycle of undernourishment" quite well by looking at what happens to a poor family that receives a full allotment of food stamps:

> Inevitably, most food-stamp families live on a nutritional cycle that starts off reasonably well, then deteriorates as the month wears on, becoming marginal if not desperate in the final week or ten days, depending on how frugal they were earlier [Lelyveld, 1985: 53].

We will return to the issue of "frugality" later when we look at actual food-stamp allotments. Lelyveld's description above suggests that *undernourishment* and the psychological strain of constant concern over the next meal is the preeminent form of hunger experienced by poor Americans. But how *harmful* is this undernourishment? The Reagan Task Force on Hunger's (1985) "Summary of Its Final Draft Report" carefully avoided this question by concentrating on the lack of any adequate indicator to measure hunger. They wrote,

> While we have found evidence of hunger in the sense that some people have difficulties with access to food, we have also found that it is at present impossible to estimate the extent of that hunger. *We cannot report on any indicator that will tell us where and by how much hunger has gone up in recent years.* But we have also found that for the vast majority of low income people, the private and public parts of the income maintenance and food assistance efforts are available and sufficient for those who take advantage of them. We have not been able to substantiate allegations of rampant hunger. We reject our inability to document the degree of "non-clinical" hunger because such lack of definitive qualitative proof contributes to a climate in which policy discussions become unhelpfully heated and unsubstantiated assertions are then substituted for hard information [p. 18; emphasis added].

This disclaimer admitting that hunger existed while being unable to document it on a statistical measure seems ingenuous except that it serves one important function—helping justify further cutbacks ($7 billion in food-stamp cutbacks between 1981-1984 alone).

Without "proof" there can be an understandable argument for no action, especially by joining that argument with condemnation of others' concerns as "unhelpfully heated." However, one month later, on February 27, 1985, the Physicians' Task Force on Hunger, made up of doctors and public-health experts, asserted in a $120,000 research study that hunger in America was at "epidemic proportions" (New York Times, 1985). While they, too, did not have one indicator that measured "where and by how much hunger has gone up in recent years," they did use several health- and nutrition-related measures that suggest an alarming problem.

First, they relied on statistics from the Census Bureau and the U.S. Department of Agriculture to determine how many people were hungry. They reasoned that the 15.5 million Americans with income below the official poverty line who do not receive food stamps are unable to get an adequate diet for at least part of every month. To that number they added subgroups of Americans living near the poverty line who also do not receive food assistance, for a total of 22.85 million, which they then rounded down to 20 million. Such numbers, it should be remembered, do not include those on welfare who do receive food stamps, nor does it question the basis by which the "poverty line" is established. (The discussion of the "poverty line" is discussed in the first chapter.) As Lelyveld (1985) suggested, many such recipients are also hungry every month.

To document their claim of an epidemic, they cited the following findings:

(1) Second Harvest, a national organization of food banks, noted a 700% increase in food distributed to pantries and soup kitchens since 1980.
(2) Clinics in poor areas reported cases of kwashiorkor and marasmus, two Third World diseases of advanced malnutrition. More prevalent, however, were cases of vitamin deficiencies, diabetes, lethargy, "stinting," "wasting," failure to thrive, and other health problems traceable to inadequate food.

Third, the U.S. infant-mortality rate is worse than that of all other industrialized nations and appears to be leveling off instead of declining. They quote an infant mortality rate of 10.9 per 1,000 live births in 1983, which is "behind that of comparably wealthy nations." The rate includes peaks as high as 25.6 per 1,000 in central Harlem in New York City. And all of these increases in hunger-related problems occurred while $12.2 billion was cut from all food-related federal programs (New York Times, 1985).

All of these figures are alarming, but none is that elusive indicator of "where and by how much" hunger has increased in the 1980s. The logic to that argument would undoubtedly not appeal to the Reagan Task Force authors if it were applied to murder: Rather than waiting to see where and by how much murder was increasing, criminologists have instead used earlier, less immediate measures of violent and criminal behavior in individuals to predict the likelihood of future violence. If they did not, they argue, there would be no way to prevent or at least minimize some violent activity until long after it had occurred.

The fallacious reasoning on hunger measures instead serves the *political purpose* of minimizing the problem while maximizing the sense of unsubstantiated assertions that emanate from those who find hunger at historically high levels. "If you figure America's hungry are less visible while a lot of other people are doing really well, it can make your political choice to cut [food stamps and nutrition programs] a lot easier to make. And that's worked a lot better than a lot of people imagined," commented one health activist recently.

THE FEDERAL FOOD PROGRAMS

The programs that have received the largest cuts—and created the largest response from food and hunger advocates—have all received widespread publicity in the 1980s. The largest and most important programs are: the Food Stamp Program, child-nutrition programs (especially school feeding programs), the Special Supplemental Program for Women, Infants, and Children (WIC), and Nutrition Programs for the Elderly.

FOOD STAMPS

By far the largest food-subsidy program is the food-stamp program, which increases the purchasing power of those using the stamps (about 35% of those eligible do not receive the stamps) (President's Task Force on Hunger, 1985). Under the original rules of the program, households were required to pay a certain amount in cash for the "bonus" they received, and were alloted in food stamps an amount calculated to meet "low-level nutritional" needs. Under current rules under attack, participating households do not pay anything for the stamps, but receive only the food stamps. Instead, they are expected to contribute from their own income a certain portion of the cost of the same basic diet. They then face the stigma of presenting the stamps at their local supermarkets whenever they use them to purchase food.

As noted earlier, $7 billion in food stamp cuts occurred between 1981-1984, with $500 to $600 million proposed for cutting in fiscal year 1986-1987. How does this all translate into its effects on the hungry? A recent fact sheet prepared by Allan Kahan of the Food and Hunger Hotline in New York City gives one an idea about how these fiscal cuts contribute to the "cycle of undernourishment." The basic *total* welfare grant was $296.70 a month for a family of four (excluding housing). The *maximum* food stamp benefit is $264.00 a month for that same family. The *average* market basket cost of food in New York was $115.74 *a week* for 4 people, as of October 4, 1984. At that rate, if a family of four received the maximum monthly amount of food stamps and the maximum basic welfare grant, there would be only $65.00 each month available for all nonfood needs (excluding housing).

At least they are fed, one might say. Not necessarily. Kahan compiled one other figure—the *average* food stamp benefit for a family receiving public assistance is $117.55—which leaves the family with a shortfall of almost $70.00 each month, assuming they bought nothing but food! Children could not have new shoelaces when old ones broke, or coats in winter, or combs for their hair. The family had better live in walking distance to schools, hospitals, welfare centers, and the shopping district, for the $2.00 round-trip fare is out of financial reach. The reality, of course, is some parents will find necessities for their children and will need to use mass transportation, so the outcome can mean only one thing—hunger at some point during each and every month. As these statistics are based on a state with one of the highest welfare grants in the nation, it is likely to be equally if not more severe for people elsewhere.

CHILD-NUTRITION PROGRAMS

These programs became most famous through the "ketchup is not a vegetable" slogan that surfaced when the Reagan Administration attempted to reclassify certain basic food commodities in the school breakfast and lunch programs as vegetables as a vehicle for cutting costs without touching broadly popular programs. A 1977 Field Foundation Report, based on testimony of physicians, reported results that show why cuts were initially so difficult:

> Our first and overwhelming impression is that there are fewer grossly malnourished people in this country today (1977) than there were 10 years ago. . . . The food stamp program, the nutritional component of Head Start, [and] school lunch and breakfast program have made the difference [Nutrition Watch, 1982: 9].

Food stamps had been easier to cut because of the still popular image of shiftless welfare cheats buying sirloin steaks with the stamps, but hungry school kids being nourished in the process of learning was another matter altogether.

Nevertheless, while ketchup did not become a vegetable, the programs were cut drastically. Under the Omnibus Budget Reconciliation Act of 1981 (OBRA), school lunch programs' subsidies per meal were reduced on full-price and reduced-price lunches, eligibility requirements were tightened, and the maximum charge on reduced-price meals was increased. For example, the cutoff point between free and reduced-price lunches was raised from 125% to 130% above the poverty line. Similar changes occurred in school breakfast and day-care center programs as well so that a 7% decrease in meals served in day care centers had occurred by 1983. The percentages sound relatively small, until one considers that the total cost reduction has been $3.5 billion.

WOMEN, INFANTS, AND CHILDREN (WIC)

This program is administered through state public-health centers. Eligibility is limited to individuals in households with gross incomes under 185% of the poverty level who are determined to be at nutritional risk by a health professional. WIC is not an entitlement program, so services are provided on a priority basis. The foods provided include fruit juices, fortified cereals, infant formula, eggs, and milk. Medical assistance and education are also provided for the 2.5 million individuals involved (as of 1983). Because of the obvious effectiveness and need of this program cuts were not made—but the expanding pool of those needing the services due to increased levels of poverty has not been reached given insufficient increases (New York Times, 1985). This is part of why the Physicians' Task Force noted increased levels in infant mortality, especially in poor urban communities.

NUTRITION SERVICES FOR THE ELDERLY

The largest single program under The Older Americans Act, begun in 1965, is the title VII "congregate dining facilities." These are the nutritional hot meals served daily to the elderly at senior citizen centers and other human-service organizations. Designed to improve nutrition and end social isolation, the total cost of the meals program was $295 million, which serviced 3 million people at 12,475 sites (Olson, 1982: 204). As large as those figures seem, these funds serve only 9% of those eligible (p. 205).

This remarkably low percentage is matched by the low numbers of seniors over 60 who receive food stamps—1.7 million, less than 5% of the aged, are served by the program (Olson, 1982: 206). That percentage has decreased since the federal budget cuts in the early 1980s.

This brief overview suggests serious problems in the food and nutrition programs that exist at the federal level. While the populations in need have been correctly identified, the level of resources is not there for *those enrolled in the programs* to avoid hunger during some part of each month. And, as the figures suggest, many of the hungry who are eligible are not even part of the programs—91% of the eligible elderly for meals programs, 35% to 40% of those eligible for food stamps, 42% of those eligible for WIC. Why?

Much of this problem lies at the doorstep—and the desks—of the welfare state. To quote the conservative Reagan Task Force (1985: 7-8):

> The net result of successive changes and modifications (in the food-stamp program) has been a burdensome system for establishing eligibility and payment levels. The determination of net income incorporates a formula with five deductions. The determination of eligibility requires the mathematical computations. Another ten decisions are required simply to determine household composition. The application and requisite worksheet cover nine pages of detailed questions.

The report goes on to suggest that this red tape leads to overpayment—an error rate of 9% a year leading to overpayment of $1 billion annually.

However, other reports suggest that this bureaucratization works in very different ways, keeping people off the rolls rather than on. New York City Comptroller Harrison Goldin reported in February 1984 that his staff did a one-week telephone survey, at random, of the 16 food-stamp offices in the city. The staff members said they needed food stamps. Of 125 calls, 38.4% went unanswered or were met with constant busy signals. Of those who did get through, a staggering 95% were given erroneous or incorrect information (New York Times, 1984). Another survey suggested one-third of New York City's poor did not receive the stamps (New York Times, 1984). Spanish-speaking applicants had the most difficulty. Meanwhile, the Food and Hunger Hotline had 15,000 calls for emergency food in the same time period, a 70% increase from the year before (U.S. News and World Report, 1984).

This problem is not located only in the "Rust Belt" of the Northeast and Midwest. One in four Texans are eligible for food stamps, with 40% of that possible pool not receiving them. Mississippi officials note that while 33% of its population is below the poverty line, only 19% receive food stamps. A month-long wait, coupled with the long forms, turns people away, the officials feel (U.S. News and World Report, 1984).

Successful application for *emergency* food stamps—needed by those so desperate that they are given food money within two to five days—has dropped by 80% under the Reagan Administration since 1981. Designed for those who are terribly indigent—households with less than $150 in monthly income and $100 in personal assets—the emergency food grant is technically part of any new welfare recipient's assistance package. But in New York, for example, of 12,500 new recipients each month, only 3,500 receive the emergency stamps. A brief survey by a New York periodical uncovered the obvious reason—a majority of welfare centers do not inform their clients that such services exist (Village Voice, November 11, 1984: 5).

How could such serious underreporting, planned discontinuation, and neglect to provide information occur? The Omnibus Reconciliation Act of 1981 included a provision that food-stamp error rates had to be reduced by 9% in fiscal year 1983, 7% by fiscal year 1984, and 5% by 1985. Under this plan, a state over the target error rate will lose 5% of federal administrative funds for each one percentage point difference between its actual error rate and the target. If the error rate is above 3%, the penalty rises to 10%. The errors, of course, are only in the direction of *overpayment* (President's Task Force on Hunger, 1985: 206). If people are erroneously kept off the rolls, their numbers are simply part of the pile that keeps the overpayment percentage down. For all its antibureaucratic stance, the administration is able to use its cumbersome food-stamp procedures as a vehicle to decrease costs that it otherwise would be forced to meet.

Besides red-tape and error-reduction penalties that reduce benefit-payment levels, other programs seem to function in a manner that trivializes and disempowers the recipients in painful ways. As Maggie Kuhn of the Grey Panthers said about the elderly nutrition programs' educational arm—"they treat seniors like wrinkled babies." With the seniors' meal programs including weekly lectures with such topics as "Let's Talk about Milk" or "Everything You Wanted to Know about Cereal" (Olson, 1982: 206), the condescension and disempowering seem obvious—and capable of deterring people fighting to maintain their dignity and self-respect.

THE PRIVATE SECTOR RESPONSE

Integral to the image of the safety net in the 1980s has been the increased involvement of the charitable, voluntary, and philanthropic organizations in food assistance. While the federal government argues that their existence "does not imply the failure of federal food assistance plans" (President's Task Force on Hunger, 1985: 11), it is important to note that the number of food pantries has increased by 2,000% since 1980 and the number of requests for food emergency through hotlines has increased 700% in a 10-year period (U.S. News and World Report, 1984). While there is "no one indicator of where and how fast" these private food programs are growing, they are now part of the American landscape in ways that have not been since the 1930s.

The purposes of these programs are as diverse as these numbers are growing. For hunger is a problem that lends itself to remarkably varied political interpretations: For some, it is a chance to "do good," to help those in need, without concerning themselves with causes for the hunger. It is enough to know that the need exists and that their soup kitchen provides relief. For others, hunger creates a moral outrage given their belief in the abundance of American life; they see their actions as part of the way to build and maintain their community. Still others see this problem as part of a growing systemic political and economic problem that is creating increasingly distinct classes of the "haves" and "have-nots." They approach such work with a desire to help those in need as a vehicle to oppose further the increasingly rightward drift in American political life.

The groups are so varied because the most salient part of the problem is so clear—food—easy to remedy, and the solution appears so obvious—get people plenty of it. If you are working with the new unemployed and set up an unemployed council, your goals for economic revitalization or even campaigns to stop utility turn-offs may take years to accomplish. With hunger, a group only needs to plan a large meal and do a little outreach and they can have results: Hungry people, from proud, thankful seniors to wondering, sad-eyed children will show up and eat.

Given people's initial motivations and concerns, you will have to think it through with your founding members before you begin operations as to what balance between direct service and longer-term advocacy you wish to achieve. Some groups have decided that they limit their advocacy to compiling records on the number of meals served, numbers turned away, etc., and passing on the results to other coalitions to use as data for wider-scale advocacy. Others join their meal or food-box preparation with advocacy for individuals; in many ways, they resemble food settlement houses at the turn of the century who compiled data on child labor through the educational services they provided in their immigrant neighborhoods. Others have members as active in wider-scale coalitions and policy work as they are in direct food distribution or meal preparation.

We want to emphasize here that the distinction between advocacy and service should not be overstated, only that the mix of the two is an important consideration for a group to make as they plan their program. Most groups, it seems, are drawn initially to the problem on an emotional level, seeing a need and wanting to help, quickly. Only later, as they see that the problem is larger and seemingly endless will they seek wider-scale advocacy. This is where skilled professionals, aware of how to work with both people's immediate perceptions of need and the longer-term, more severe nature of the problem, are invaluable. Let us assume you will take responsibility for organizing or participating in such a group. Your combination of openness and expertise can go far in helping a group join both advocacy and service together more quickly.

You will have an idea of what your group wants to do by the type of program it seems to establish. Food banks are so large that they will not be considered in detail here. They will be discussed below as a backdrop to the three more common food and hunger groups: emergency food centers, food-distribution programs, and soup

kitchens. As a general rule, the less time spent on direct food preparation, the higher the degree of advocacy and interest in coalition
work around food policy.

Food banks deal with large-volume and bulky purchases and
donations at a citywide or regional level. Utilizing federal tax laws
passed in 1976 that make voluntary food contributions tax deductible, these food banks deal primarily with food companies and
supermarket chains. They then store the products until they are
distributed to community-based feeding programs. Almost all of
them are affiliated with Second Harvest, the national food-bank
network (Second Harvest Newsletter, August 1983). As there are
over 70 food banks in the country at this writing, there is probably
one relatively near your community, especially if it is in an urban
area. It is relatively easy to affiliate with a bank that does exist, if
your group conforms to a few consistent rules. Your pantry or soup
kitchen must be a nonprofit organization that is currently operating
established on-site meal or food-distribution programs. Secondly,
the food bank *cannot* be your only source of food because it can
distribute only what donations it receives, which can vary widely
on a weekly basis. A balanced selection of foods is not guaranteed
and is the responsibility of your own community operation.

Operationally, your group will have to call once a week to order
food from the bank's inventory. A certain price per pound of food
ordered is required to offset maintenance costs (in 1985, usually 9¢
to 15¢ a pound). Groups must pick up their own food, which means
you must have enough trucks, vans, or cars available, which can be
a hardship for groups just starting out. Make certain you have your
transportation worked out early. Some pantries or kitchens in neighboring areas pool resources or van or truck rentals to lessen costs.

THE VOLUNTEER PROGRAMS

There are many similarities in the planning and running of all
other food programs: determining community needs, organizing
a committee, raising funds, recruiting volunteers, establishing a
board of directors, and selecting a site. The end of this chapter
spells out this process in detail for the reader to use. All of this is
part of your operation and will probably take more time than you
initially expected. Plan on at least three months before you open
your doors. Fund raising and recruiting volunteers, as well as publicity, are the three ongoing outreach functions that your group

would be involved in consistently past the preplanning stage. Volunteers are most consistently drawn from religious groups, civic organizations, schools, and other service organizations. These groups are important in your needs assessment as well, meeting with them and public social-service organizations to ascertain needs and to minimize the duplication of already existing programs. By establishing firm links with them early on, you have a more ready referral source, pool of volunteers, and publicity chain that will keep your program visible to the public.

Site selection and board membership are preplanning activities that will not need as much repetition but need to be done carefully. Your site should not be located too closely to others nor far removed from where the hungry live; at the same time it should not be too difficult for volunteers to reach. Likewise, the actual site—from a church or synagogue's basement to a community center's old recreation room—will label your own program in ways that your own group should be comfortable with. Make certain you know of and are pleased with the site sponsor's community reputation before you move in.

Your board members' reputations should be equally compatible with your group's philosophy. Usually, most food programs seek board members who are well known, represent established groups and constituencies (from labor unions to civic associations) and, not insignificantly, have genuine interest with food-related issues. Some of the organizing committee are also part of the board, and most groups make certain one attorney is a member. It is their job to establish by-laws and review the long-term policy and objectives of the program, while daily activities are left to program activists, volunteers, and paid staff (if there are any).

These similarities in program design and function are joined with some modest but evident differences. Soup kitchens obviously need a kitchen; food-box programs need more shelf and storage space. In general, a soup kitchen will need a paid or permanently involved person preparing meals and an ongoing number of volunteers at each meal: The emphasis will be on food preparation and immediate distribution. Food-box programs will need (usually) a paid nutritionist to establish what can go in food boxes to families and individuals in need, but the volunteers are needed more for outreach, food collection, and storage, which can be done on different schedules and varied hours of the day. Fewer trained personnel are needed for distribution than either meal preparation or its cleanup. The kitchens will be more hectic during the limited mealtime hours, while the food-box programs will be less hectic but are more likely to go for longer hours of the day.

These differences are a matter of degree, but in general one's choice of program will influence the degree of advocacy one's group can perform. As the above operations suggest, a soup kitchen is more insular and inner focused. There's a lot to do to get meals prepared, distributed, eaten, and cleaned up after. It can be exciting yet intense work each day. That is why many soup kitchens often seek what are called "caterers"—voluntary civic or religious groups whose members take responsibility for one weekly meal or one day's meals. Such catering lessens the burden of any one group to maintain the hectic pace demanded in kitchens. At the same time, this means that its volunteers are unlikely to view their work past the meal itself.

Box programs, with the constant need of publicity and outreach to sources of food, the utilization of food drives to engage new volunteers and replenish supplies, and the slower pace of actual distribution, will by definition be focused more outward. Such an outward focus, which demands consistent discussion and mention of the hungry in one's community, opens up these programs to more advocacy.

This is why relatively more food-box programs start to function like Emergency Food Centers (EFCs), which provide not only a three-day emergency food package but also (1) information and prescreening for food stamps; (2) nutrition counseling; (3) budget counseling; and (4) referrals to agencies. This work is done in conjunction with existing (usually public) services. But EFCs also often come to serve three other functions as well: (a) advocacy counseling on behalf of recipients; (b) monitoring of existing agencies; (c) researching the extent of hunger in the community. As the author of one booklet wrote, "An EFC can be more than a brief oasis in a long and trying struggle for survival; it can become a vehicle for aid and an effective base in the community from which to attack hunger" (Food Monitor, 1979: 17).

These programs will also call for more professional skill (except in terms of nutrition, which is very important in soup-kitchen meal preparation). Volunteers must be trained in solid nutritional information, knowing how to evaluate adequate dietary needs *given the food available for the recipient*. It is not enough to know one should have a mix of protein, complex carbohydrates, grains and fruit, all spiced with vitamin supplements, when a family's food box is heavy on canned goods. A nutritionist will be needed for such training to make certain that volunteers don't present unrealistic and demoralizing expectations to people whose immediate provisions obviously cannot meet high-level desires. Counseling and individual advocacy for clients will necessitate training in entitlement legislation, from welfare to food stamps. The 10 pages of forms and emergency-relief needs mentioned earlier in this chapter will need to be understood by anyone wishing to advocate effectively with these programs' recipients.

Such work in advocacy training is often available through public welfare organizations and other not-for-profit groups concerned with entitlements. It demands not only familiarity with the rules but some experience in regulating the bureaucratic systems of food stamps and welfare centers. This kind of experience can only be gained as you assist others. Such experience will also bring you in contact with a number of once "faceless bureaucrats," some of whom in fact, will be supportive, involved, and committed people. These people become valuable allies in one's march through regulations.

The nature of their work may mean they cannot respond to every request, but used judiciously they can be valuable allies in your fight for a center recipient's entitlements or other services. Once real trust has been established, these few can be counted on to pass on formal and informal information related to new or proposed procedures, policy recommendations, etc. That can help food and hunger advocates in their broader-scale organizing/advocacy work.

Broader-scale organizing and advocacy among food and hunger activists depends on one vital tool of soup kitchens and food-box programs alike: record keeping. Hunger and its attendant needs, because they superficially appear less glaring than in other parts of the world, need constant documentation to validate that people are not eating enough each month, and that many do not have sufficient nutritious food available to maintain a healthy and robust life. Without these statistics, ketchup would now be a vegetable, and the national Physician's Task Force would not have had the data available to argue about an "epidemic of hunger" in the United States. This data-collection skill is important in your program's functioning.

One can see the exciting potential in "working under the safety net" when one considers how effectively many groups have been in pooling their information together: Each soup kitchen and every food-box program monitors its numbers of recipients, numbers turned away, amount of food given, etc., and larger-scale advocacy groups have tallied the combined figures to undercut effectively arguments against increased food programs in America. While not able to stem the conservative tide in this country against many social-welfare cutbacks, it is clear their presence limited some of the damage.

This network of groups, working at myriad tasks in a variety of settings, begins to shape an image of the kind of coalitions emerging in the late 1980s. To some, the work may go no further than placing food on another's empty plate; for others it is full-time advocacy, organizing, and fund raising. If similar objectives are understood, each can see they help the other in their tasks. But there are two potential pitfalls that anyone involved in food and hunger must be aware of in this work.

The first is competition between groups over both economic resources and political turf. Food programs are almost always in need of money and food: the money to take care of staffing needs, rent, office supplies, and other operating costs (from kitchen utensils to per-diem gasoline allowances). Initial seed money for a soup kitchen in smaller communities runs about $3,000 in 1985; larger communities need over $10,000. Likewise, relations with those providing the food itself—supermarkets, warehouse chains, smaller shops, church and civic groups that take on a weekly or monthly commitment—need to be established and maintained. Both needs run the risk of overlapping or competing with other groups. Your fund-raising and food-resource work needs to be worked out carefully so as to minimize resentment and in-fighting with groups that need to be allies. This can be done in part by seeking your foodstuffs from organizations not already affiliated with other groups or from public programs where proven need is the primary basis for selection. It is also possible for groups to coordinate food drives, "walks against hunger," and other publicity drives and then to split the proceeds.

Fund raising from foundations is a bit trickier and needs to be explored in great detail by any group serious about maintaining itself (Lauffer, 1985). The simplest way to minimize the competition is to develop sectors of your program for particular populations not being adequately serviced in your community (e.g., the elderly home bound, the very young, etc.) and then approach foundations, religious groups, etc., who are interested in these groups. You may also have a particularly distinct manner in how you do your work that they would be interested in. Realistically, however, you may end up competing for funds from the other, equally involved groups. If this occurs, emphasize the positive about your group and not the negative about others. This can keep friction at more tolerable levels.

The second problem is one of political turf, where some organizations seek to preempt other groups from leadership and then use their reputation to increase both funding potential and the personal recognition for their leaders. Nothing undermines the possibility of effective network and coalition building more than such battles over turf. The outcome of such turf battles (by no means unique to "food and hunger" groups) is the effective sabotaging of group efforts around wide-scale advocacy, legislative work, and effective citywide and statewide monitoring of public efforts. It is unfortunate in the late 1980s that groups commonly united around stopping cuts in social welfare still engage in this type of in-fighting for leadership over an already shrinking pie. Such maneuvers can be limited by developing coalitional structures described elsewhere (Burghardt, 1982: chap. 7), but each new group should be aware of these dangers so it works to limit their influence inside their own networking.

While these dangers are real, the overwhelming amount of work by volunteers in soup kitchens, food-box programs, emergency food centers, and hotlines is productive and helpful in lessening the anguish of hundreds of thousands of people weekly. While not enough to end hunger or lessen its overall rate of increase, the programs so many are involved in are of great importance. These efforts, almost always joined with a cheerful commitment to "help" that creates a supportive and open environment for those in need, suggests the best in the voluntary impulse.

What follows are three appendices that outline some fundamental programs and plans for setting up food and hunger programs. They give the reader interested in the issue an immediate tested vehicle to begin work in this area. Those are: the scheduling of events in setting up a soup kitchen or emergency food-box program; a checklist of all important work to be done before such a program actually opens; finally, the third appendix explains what to do to set up an emergency food center, with its greater emphasis on how to become known to the public and with the referral agencies in the community. After these appendices come a few personal and programmatic issues for people to answer before the work begins. Don't forget—food is an emotional and political issue for worker and recipient alike; your group's decisions on both how to train members and how to receive recipients will affect your program's reputation immensely.

APPENDIX 1:
Schedule of Events[1]

Event/accomplishment	Resources	Time Frame
(1) Volunteers		
—Recruit, organize, train	Questionnaire	Early in planning stage
—Work assignments, position descriptions	Word of mouth Church bulletins	Ongoing activity
—Coordinator position description	Newspaper	
(2) Funding		
—Proposal for seed money	Foundations, churches, companies	Within two months
—Donations	Businesses, churches, community organizations, state charitable bureau	
—Fund raising events	Walk for hunger	
(3) Site selection		Within 2 to 3 months
—Contact realtors	Community realtors	Allow 3 to 6 months to
—Check known facilities	Community centers, City Community Development office	locate suitable site
—Determine renovations		
—Donate/purchase equipment	Health Department	
—Services	City Hall, Building Dept.	
—Lease	Attorney	Allow 3 to 6 months to
—Building permit	Chamber of Commerce	renovate

Event/accomplishment	Resources	Time Frame
(4) Board of Directors	Committee members, attorney, community volunteers	Within 1 to 5 months
—Vote and establish		
—Incorporate		
—Develop by-laws	Incorporate with Secretary of State Corporation Div.	
—Develop board responsibilities		
—Philosophy	Tax exemption: IRS, attorney	
—Logo		
—Nonprofit tax exemption	Chamber of Commerce	Allow 3 to 6 months to renovate
(5) Budget		
—Paid/salary coordinator	Attorney	Early in planning stage
—Profit/loss statements	Board treasurer	

—Salary, fringe benefits, food, equipment, disposables, freight, travel, rent/lease, utilities, insurance, repairs, phone

Ongoing activity

—Income, funds

(6) Food service

—Hot/cold food	Coordinator	Prior to site selection
—Equipment	Nutritionist	
—Utensils	Home economist	
—Disposables/dishes	Equipment companies	
—Type service	Salvage outlets	
—Hours, days, meals	Restaurant owners	
—Caterers	Businesses	
—Coordinator, paid/salary	Other soup kitchens	
	Cooperative extension (USDA)	

(7) Public relations and publicity

—Promote community support and interest — Address church groups, civic organizations, Mayor's office, Salvation Army, Welfare offices — Public Relations during organizing phase and ongoing

—Media coverage — Local newspapers — Publicity, organizing phase, kitchen opening, ongoing
—Public hearings — Chamber of Commerce

APPENDIX 2:
Check List

Use this list to be sure you have covered all points.

_____ Needs assessment

_____ Community interest
_____ Organizing committee
_____ Meet with community

_____ Hold information or community meetings
_____ Recruit volunteers, questionnaires
_____ Train volunteers
_____ Develop a proposal for seed money

_____ Building permit and materials
_____ Health permit
_____ Utility costs
_____ Paid coordinator, possibly a chef
_____ Soup-kitchen rules

_____ Coordinator responsibilities/training
_____ Sanitation
_____ Work assignments for volunteers

_____ Budget and establish goal   _____ Police coverage
_____ Hold fund-raising events   _____ Coordinator's name and
                                           number to police
_____ Donations of money and   _____ Frequent meetings to dis-
      services   cuss problems
_____ Thank-you notes   _____ Cafeteria, family-style, or
                                           waitress service
_____ Establish board of direc-   _____ Disposable or dishes
      tors
_____ Elect officials   _____ Utensils, tables, and chairs
_____ Develop board official   _____ Institutional-size equipment,
      responsibilities   refrigeration
_____ Incorporate   _____ Hot meals or luncheon type
_____ Obtain nonprofit mail   _____ Number of days open
      permit
_____ Develop by-laws   _____ Number of meals per day
_____ Board training   _____ Hours
_____ Join Chamber of Com-   _____ Sources of food donations
      merce as nonprofit agency
_____ Establish a philosophy   _____ Extermination
_____ Site selection   _____ Laundry
_____ Zoning   _____ Repairs
_____ Realtors services   _____ Adequate storage
_____ Lease, space, rent, loca-
      tion, insurance
_____ Renovations   _____ Media coverage
_____ Lawyer, architect, con-
      tractor

APPENDIX 3:
EFC How-To

I. THE NEED AND THE RESPONSE

If you want to establish an EFC, you will need to answer two
questions:
   —Does your community need one?
   —Does an EFC or some group like it exist in your community?
There are a number of local groups you can call to find out the
answers to these questions:
   —welfare department;
   —police department;
   —churches;

—hospitals;
—fraternal organizations.

It is good to contact these groups early on, for they make up the backbone of the referring agencies to any EFC. It is extremely good public relations to involve them in the initial planning.

If you find there is a group doing similar work to what you are planning, spend some time with them to learn what you can and determine if:

—they are doing all that you would do;
—you should join forces with them and strengthen the overall endeavor.

It is wasteful to duplicate any currently existing organization that is successfully doing the job.

II. ORGANIZING

When you are convinced of the need for an EFC, you will need support:

—First, talk to people you think might be interested: church people, members of food, hunger, and nutrition groups, community organizations, fraternal groups, poor people, etc. Tell them what you are planning.
—Then, call together interested people for a series of meetings to begin the organizing process. Practically speaking, the organizing group should not be too large, certainly not over 15 people.

When the organizing group meets, be sure everyone is in basic agreement about what an Emergency Food Center is and what it can and cannot do. Discuss its fundamental function of immediate aid. Consider also the potential role as counselor for the person who comes to the center as well as those roles that can arise from the information you will be receiving: monitoring or existing agencies and uncovering hunger in your area.

With this discussion in mind, there are other areas that need consideration: starting level, resources, and policy.

A. Starting Level

You will need to make an initial determination of how big your operation will be when you start. Some questions to ask are:

— What is the geographic area you will (should) be covering?
— Who should be on the advisory board?
   • Will one person take the lead? One organization?
   • Who will do what?

- Where will responsibilities lie?
— Are you going to rely on volunteers or a paid staff? In either case, some traits to look for in a coordinator are:
  - one-to-one work experience with people;
  - public speaking experience;
  - self-motivation;
  - church/synagogue/civic experience and connections;
  - writing ability;
  - organizational/management ability;
  - a good sense of humor.
— How many people do you estimate will need to use the service?
— How much food in stock do you want to start with?
— What hours will you be open?

B. RESOURCES
What resources are available to you:
Location: where will you be? Picking a suitable site is of critical importance. Your earlier considerations of how large a start to make may depend on what's available here.
— Consider the transportation needs of the people you want to serve. Is it centrally located? Is it easily accessible by public transportation?
— Consider the transportation requirements of your food resources. Are you close to your supply?
— Investigate all sources of free or low-cost space: churches, store fronts, county or town buildings, garages. (A workable size is 20′ by 12′—the size of the average church schoolroom.)

Food resources: This is of prime importance. You must be sure of a regular supply, you will need some responsible disbursement procedures, you will need some (even minimal) accounting procedures (especially for funding and documentation purposes). Try to develop a rotating schedule of food donations to ensure a constant supply. Consider:
— Does your community have a food bank?
— Do you have (potential) cooperating churches for food drives?
— Do you have (potential) cooperating referral agencies?
— How about contributions from corporations?
— How will you get the food? Will the source deliver?

Financial Resources: Do you have money to hire a paid coordinator or to give cash disbursements to recipients?

— Develop a budget to cover your essential costs: rent, personnel, telephone, utilities, fuel, transportation.
— If any of those are donated, keep a record of their worth.

C. POLICY

You will need to make some basic decisions about policy:
— Referrals
  • will you accept people who come in off the street?
  • or only from referral agencies?
  • who will you accept as referring agencies?

Face squarely your relationship with the Department of Public Assistance (Social Services, Welfare). Develop a policy and make sure the agencies understand it. Visit them and discuss frankly your availability and limitations. It is not to your benefit or theirs if you get swamped and discouraged out of existence.

— Do you accept or want cash for emergency distribution? (For example, to someone without cooking facilities.)

What kind of food are you going to give out? How long a period will it cover? 1, 2, 3 days? This will influence your stockpiling needs.

Are you interested in an all-volunteer operation? Or paid staff? Or a combination? If you are going to rely on many volunteers, consider the need for continuity of service as volunteers come and go.

— What sort of accounting will you have as a minimum and as an ideal? It is important to keep accurate documentation both of the effectiveness of the various public agencies and the degree of hunger and malnourishment in your community. This information can provide some of the material for funding as well as basic data for legislative changes.

III. GO TO WORK!

Once you have a coordinator, a site and any necessary funding, and have decided basic policy, begin. The following is an eight-week plan of action that might prove useful to you as you get ready to open to the public.

Six to Eight Weeks Ahead

— Develop a simple referral procedure.
— Start soliciting food:

- set up speaking engagements at churches to publicize what you are doing and ask for their support;
- plan a "food raiser"—i.e., a food day;
- contact likely community organizations and corporations.

— Get the physical space in order. Put up shelving for food storage.

— Develop an inventory system.

— Meet with a nutritionist and develop a list of foods you will ask for.

Four to Six Weeks Ahead

— Alert all potential referral agencies (churches and others) by letter:
  - ask for suggestions;
  - seek food drives;
  - ask for special training from appropriate agencies on such items as food-stamp screening and welfare procedures;
  - ask for predictions of need by the agencies;
  - investigate transportation; will the agency be able to pick up the food if the person cannot?

— As your assessment of needs progresses, start to recruit volunteers but do not recruit until you have a specific task for them to do.
  - possible sources for volunteers include the churches (especially those you have contacted); youth training programs; senior citizen centers; boy/girl scouts; interested people from agencies.
  - set up a volunteer training program.

— Decide on the make-up of the food package.

— Design a system keeping track of:
  - where people live;
  - who referred them;
  - why they have come;
  - what is the family composition;
  - how many times they have sought emergency help.

Two to Four Weeks Ahead

— Send referral information to all potential sources. Include your opening date. This packet should contain:
  - a referral "how-to" sheet;
  - a food request sheet;
  - a list of foods that will be given.
— Contact as many churches/synagogues as possible to finalize plans for food drives:
  - arrange for food pick-up and delivery;
  - arrange for volunteers to stock and sort food.
— Start collecting supermarket bags and boxes.
— Plan your public-relations approach. Consider carefully your PR task. If you go to the public, you may get more people than you can handle

Zero to Two Weeks Ahead

— Continue collecting food.
— Call each referral agency one week before opening to confirm that referral materials have been received, to answer any questions on referral procedures, and to be sure you have the name of a contact person in the agency.
— Offer training in referral to any agency that requests assistance.

IV. LOOKING AT THE RESULTS

Once you have opened your doors, keep track of everything. Your information will give you the clues you need to respond effectively. You may be swamped. If you are, review your information:

— Where are most people coming from? Maybe another EFC can be set up there. Look for allies in that part of your community.
— Can you handle more food where you are? Check your resources and let them know your needs. Let the media know, too. Who knows, you may find new donors.

If no one comes forward, check through the whole procedure to determine what has gone wrong. For example, your determination of community need may not be accurate; your location may be inaccessible or intimidating. Or the referral agencies may not be using you. Find out why.

Or, you may have planned just right, according to capacity. Again, review your information:
- — Do you want to expand? Should you link up with other communities?
- — If there is no food bank, is one feasible? If so, start planning.
- — Start thinking about more than food relief; think about moving into advocacy, monitoring, and documentation.

Questions to Consider
Personal
- — How do you react to hungry people? Do you get angry or frustrated if they are too needy? Too passive? Do you help immediately without regard to circumstance?
- — How do you react to overweight people? Do you tend to think they just eat too much, or have you learned to see the role that starch plays in poor people's diets: The same issues apply when you see people with poor skin complexions—how do you respond?

Policy
- — (See Appendix 3 under "policy" for other important questions)
- — How do you define the food problem? How does your group?
- — Do you see it as an individual, moral, or political economic problem?
- — Does your group tolerate disagreement over these issues?
- — Does your group plan educationals for its own members on this topic?
- — Is there a consistent attempt by the group made to connect hunger to other social problems of the day (like jobs, housing, etc.)? Is it consciously encouraged? Discouraged?
- — Do professional human-service workers play different roles from volunteers? How extreme are the differences? Is there effort put into skill development on the part of volunteers?

NOTE

1. *Food Monitor* (1979). The appendix and checklist are drawn from *Food Monitor's* work. Their journal is invaluable for food and hunger activists.

Chapter 4

OLDER AMERICANS

Betty and Marshall B., 78 years old, live in their own home in a medium-sized industrial town in New England. He, a retired pipe fitter, and she, a former grade-school teacher, live comfortably on two pensions, Social Security, and other modest savings and investments. Their home is paid for, and after retirement they purchased the small house next door as an investment. Marshall square dances three nights a week, often at the senior center, for which he works part time as a bus driver. Betty, while less active than he, makes the meals and is content to "keep house." All in all, a secure and satisfying life for two older Americans in 1986.

Down in Charlottsville, Virginia, Gertie M. was recently faced with a different set of circumstances. At 73, diabetic, nearly deaf, and with a newly amputated right leg, she was told by a hospital worker that her bed was no longer available. Her Medicare, she was informed, had run out. Returning home seemed impossible. Her elderly husband was too frail to care for her, and the house had no running water.

Brought home by ambulance attendants who simply placed her in a chair and left, Gertie started to lose control of her bladder. Her social worker, who had rushed to the house upon hearing of her abrupt discharge, found her sitting in urine. Within one hour of discharge her wound needed dressing and her insulin shot was overdue. It would be at least one month before a home-care worker could be provided. Desperate to help, the social worker asked her boss to intervene at a local nursing home. Gertie was placed within the week. Some who knew her case considered her fortunate (Fergin, 1985).

These two scenarios represent the parallel realities of older Americans. For many, old age has had a degree of financial stability and personal self-sufficiency that would have seemed impossible 25 years ago. For others, old age has been little better than a prison without walls. Isolated, impoverished, and frail, they live from day to day with neither financial independence nor self-sufficiency in their latter years.

We will explore these parallel worlds of the aged in this chapter, for both exist. The 1980s have been harsh to many social groups, but it is not possible to say that as uniformly when we discuss older Americans. At the same time, there are changes within the nature and delivery of both entitlements and services that have begun to turn hard-fought gains of the old into abusive forms of disengagement from their most pressing needs. As we shall see, if it were not for the ongoing political activity, mobilization, and self-help efforts of older Americans and their allies, their conditions would be much worse.

BACKGROUND CHARACTERISTICS

The economic situation of the elderly has improved dramatically in the last two decades. As late as 1961, census data revealed that more than one-third of the elderly—6 million people—were in poverty. Between 1960 and 1970, this number decreased to 5.7 million, about a 5% drop. Between 1970 and 1985, the number is below 4 million, a decrease of 50% (Burt and Pittman, 1985: 117). Given that the number of people over 65 has increased 54% from 16.6 million in 1960 to 25.6 million in 1980, these numbers are impressive.

Perhaps more significantly, the economic situation of older Americans has improved in relative as well as absolute terms. As late as 1970, over 25% of elderly Americans were below the poverty line, compared to 12.6% for the entire population. In 1981, 14% of the total population and 15.3% of the elderly were classified as poor; in 1983, this situation was almost reversed. For the first time, older Americans were marginally less poor than those under 65 (Burt and Pittman, 1985: 117).

These gains, when considered in the context of budget deficits, inflation, and reduced domestic spending, have led some to argue that most of the elderly do not need more federal assistance (Neugarten, 1982). Consistent with other popular appeals to scale back the welfare state to only the "truly needy," this argument seeks to move away from *age-based* policies to *need-based* policies.

As we will show later in this chapter, this argument ignores certain structural flaws within the two most preeminent entitlements of the elderly, Social Security, and Medicare. Important to note here, however, are the demographic trends among older Americans. The populations most at risk among the old are those growing most rapidly. The number of Americans between 65 and 74 has doubled since 1950; the number of "older" elderly (74+) has risen 150% during the same time period, from 4 to 10 million. In 1950, there were equal proportions of elderly men and women; in 1980 there were 3 older women for every 2 men (U.S. Bureau of the Census, 1984). While in absolute numbers still small, black and Hispanic life spans have begun to increase as well. As for living arrangements, while for men things have not changed since the 1950s, the percentage of isolated older women has risen from 19% to 42%. (Perhaps surprisingly, the percentage of women living with spouses is the same since 1960, while the proportion living with children or other relatives has dropped from 23% to 11%.) In short, the groups of elderly who benefited the least from federal efforts of the explosive 1970s and 1980s are expected to make up an increasingly larger proportion of the older population of the 1990s and beyond.

SOCIAL SECURITY

The looming problems of the elderly poor are obscured at present in the more popular debate over Social Security that has been led by conservative forces since 1976. Picked up by the popular press and reified into assumed objective truth, these arguments suggest that in general the elderly have become comfortable through a program that is sapping our federal budget, has become "actuarially unsound," and "forces present day workers to unfairly pay for older workers' benefits." Not surprisingly, these arguments usually conclude with calls for an end to Social Security cost-of-living adjustments, increasing the age at which one can begin collecting benefits, and, of course, replacing overutilization of Social Security with private pension plans (Myers, 1981).

These arguments make it appear as if social security were quite a fiscal elephant, out of control. Analysts 20 years ago wrote differently. One liberal wrote:

In no other welfare system in the world did the state shirk all its responsibilities for old-age indigency and insist that funds be taken out of the current earnings of workers. By relying on regressive taxation (the payroll tax) and withdrawing vast sums to build up reserves, the act did untold economic mischief. The law denied coverage to numerous classes of workers, notably farm laborers and domestics [Leuchtenberg, 1963: 32].

We will look below at some of the issues raised in the above quotations, especially the payroll tax and coverage. It is presented here as a reminder of how thoroughly today's dominant political perceptions have shifted the Social Security debate. John Myers, rather than simply rehashing old debates, developed a thoughtful analysis that explodes all neoconservative myths succinctly (Myers, 1981). American Social Security, the least generous of state pension plans of any industrialized nation,[1] was devised in the Great Depression to meet the consumption needs of the old *and* as a mechanism that would draw workers out of the labor market (and thus reduce unemployment). In short, while newer workers pay into this system through payroll taxes, older workers reciprocated by leaving their jobs for younger replacements.

Payroll taxes are, of course, regressive taxes, that is, they are flat-rate taxes that remove a disproportionately larger share from workers' wages than from corporations or upper-income individuals. Employers match the amount given to the fund by each of their workers. While regressive in social terms, it is a relatively nonbureaucratized, pay-as-you-go system. Rather than paying into a capital fund that generated interest and benefits, current expenditures (Social Security checks) are paid out of current revenues (payroll taxes). This made the system almost immediately operable—an important consideration in the 1930s and prescient when looking at the 1980s. Social Security, as large as it is, has had nothing to do with the federal deficit: Its revenues and its expenditures are separately earmarked. They have had a surplus since its beginning, regardless of doomsayers' past predictions. As one member of Congress in Washington remarked, "Trying to cut Social Security because of the deficit is like telling you not to water your lawn because there's an oil shortage." Like oil and water, Social Security and federal deficits don't mix.

As discussed in Chapter 1, capitalism's crisis in investment and profitability lie behind the conservative's attack on the welfare state. While Social Security has little to do with deficits, corporate payroll tax reductions could add to investment funds otherwise unavailable. Conservatives understand this. Recognizing the shifting demographics in an aging population, they have latched on to this "pay-as-you-go" system as "actuarially unsound," an ominous phrase used for *private market firms* when their present assets are below future economic obligations (long-term debt, outstanding loans, and so on). However, Social Security as even Reagan economist Martin Feldstein (1977) has noted, is not a private market program. It is a state system whose "soundness" rests on the state's ability to collect taxes. As Feldstein (p. 90) wrote, "as long as the voters support the Social Security System, it will be able to pay the benefits it promises."

Thus, the system's soundness is a political, not financial question. Will younger generations create a taxpayer's revolt against the elderly? In 1980-1981, the combined employee-employer Social Security tax rate on covered earnings was 13%; it will rise to 15.5% by 1990. These are modest rates compared to other countries. In 1978, the combined tax rate in Italy was 24%; 20.3% in Sweden, 18% in West Germany.

Popular arguments to the contrary, neither potential actuarial problems nor momentous demographic shifts seem to exist. Indeed, in looking at western European societies that are already "old" by demographic standards, there are no political clashes between retirees and young workers. The elderly already constitute 16% of the population of Austria, Sweden, and West Germany, which is not far from the 18% at which the American elderly population is expected to peak in the next century. They have higher pensions than in the United States, and are financed by younger workers whose standard of living is considerably lower than that of Americans. If they have not done battle yet, there is little reason to raise the spectre of intergenerational conflict here—except as a vehicle to create that conflict.

Perhaps one of the primary reasons why there has been so little organized support from working people behind these conservative fears is their personal comparisons with privately sponsored pension plans for working people.

A quick review of private pension plans (Thompson, 1978) shows that private occupational plans do not compare well with Social Security. While paid for by the employer, they are commonly agreed by economists to be "deferred wages" that are traded off for present wages and benefits (Myers, 1981: 27). Unfortunately, workers lose these deferred wages when they lose or change jobs. Unless these pension credits have been vested, the money reverts to the employer. Prior to the Employment Retirement Income Security Act of 1974 (ERISA), vesting was virtually nonexistent. By 1979, 42% of active workers were in this program; only 25% were vested. The danger of losing those deferred wages has been quite real for them, given the increasingly precarious job security faced by American working people. No such problem with Social Security exists.

The actual dollar value of Social Security is far greater than almost all private plans. The latter programs are fixed in "nominal" dollars, while Social Security benefits are fixed in "real" dollars. Social Security is adjusted to inflation so that over the life of the individual he or she experiences no net loss in these benefits. Finally, Social Security has built-in survivor's benefits after the worker's death—benefits that few private plans provide.

It is therefore no accident that Social Security remains popular with Americans—there has been no alternative to match it for the vast majority of working people, young and old. Social Security neither has created federal-budget deficits nor is financially dangerous to the vast majority of working people. There have been at least 17 attempts since 1980 to roll back Social Security cost-of-living adjustments and other provisions of the act. With the exception of one six-month delay in cost-of-living increases in 1983, almost all significant cutbacks have failed as politicians, recognizing the concerns of older and younger voters alike, have been afraid to alter the most popular entitlement in the history of the American welfare state.

As real as its popularity and benefits are, there are serious problems in Social Security that are emerging with even greater intensity in the 1980s. They have little to do with neoconservative arguments or fears and much more to do with implicit class, gender, and racial inequities found within the program.

As Olson (1982: 6) documents, Social Security replaces a certain percentage of earned income for every worker, with lower-wage workers receiving a higher percentage than those at the upper-income levels. As equitable as that seems, however, these replacement ratios apply to "average monthly indexed earnings" over a worker's lifetime and apply only to retirees and dependent spouses who receive their initial pensions at age 65. If they retire earlier—as lower-income workers more often do—they do not qualify. Furthermore, Social Security is organized where the highest benefits in practice accrue to these employees within each income group who have had long and continuous places of employment. For those either disabled at an earlier age—disproportionately black and Hispanic—or intermittently in the labor force—again, either people of color or women with childcare responsibilities—their potential benefits are consistently lower (Olson, 1982: chap. 2). Thus, in 1979, 46% of all retired workers had an average Social Security benefit under $3,360 a year.

Unquestionably, however, the 1980s have not been as harmful to the elderly of all income strata as some might have expected. One study (Moom and Sawhill, 1984) reported, "Over the 1980-84 period, the disposable income of families headed by someone sixty-five or older rose by 9.5 percent—nearly three times the increase for all families. Older individuals living alone had greater gains—their incomes rose about 15%. . . . Even the bottom 20 percent had income increases of about six percent" (Moom and Sawhill, 1984).

As rosy as these figures seem, the elderly poor who receive Supplemental Security Income have not been as fortunate, as Burt and Pittman (1985) note. This program was to be the answer to the dilemma to provide a guaranteed minimum for the low-income elderly while not benefiting those with other significant income sources. However, SSI benefits have been outstripped by Social Security itself. Between 1975 and 1981, for example, Social Security benefits went up 19%, while SSI for the elderly dropped 4%. The number of elderly SSI recipients qualifying first as "aged" dropped 22%, while the number of Social Security recipients increased by about that amount (Burt and Pittman, 1985: 131). One could argue the latter program balanced the former, were it not for the fact that 87% of the elderly living below the poverty line in 1981 were Social Security recipients.

This means that a significant number of elderly receive Social Security benefits that are too high to allow them to collect SSI, but too low to escape poverty. Instead of the 4.6 million eligible elderly poor receiving SSI, only 1.7 million received it in 1981. These numbers are not increasing in the latter 1980s. Equally important, not being on SSI means a possible loss of medical coverage through Medicaid as well. Losing Medicaid eligibility entails a loss of resources to pay the recipients' deductible under Medicaid. As Medicare deductibles since 1975 have risen over 140%—$420 in 1986—uncovered, short-term health costs now account for 18% of the *total* annual benefits (SS, SSI, Medicaid, etc.), of the elderly person receiving minimum payments. Equivalent problems are occurring in subsidized housing programs that have been cut back (Burt and Pittman, 1985: 137-138).

What all these figures speak to is the increasing problems and financial pressures for a significant group of elderly that have existed and continue to exist in the 1980s. At the same time, this group's concerns have been almost invisible given the relative progress for so many older Americans over the last eight years, progress that seems all the more pronounced because so many other populations' problems have intensified.

As we will see in the last section of this chapter, this success against cutbacks was not out of simple official generosity. It occurred due to concerted political and organizing actions of older Americans and their allies. This activism, however, has not been completely successful in protecting all of the elderly on a number of issues. For example, the Older Americans Act of 1965, so important in the development of senior centers, has been cut greatly (Burt and Pittman, 1985: 139-141). But we can see this most strikingly when we look at the attack on Medicare.

THE ENSNARING ATTACK ON OLDER AMERICANS: MEDICARE AND DRGs

The attacks against Social Security have failed in part because of well-mobilized political opposition. Nevertheless, there is also another material reason for why conservative leaders have not been able to free up more funds for corporate-investment purposes (cutting SS cannot erode the deficit as was explained earlier in this chapter). Social Security is far more uniformly structured into the fabric of American life than is Medicare. Social Security involves 93% of all Americans who are or have been part of the labor force; Medicare is an entitlement for older Americans alone. Social Security has the appearance of a pension program, with the positive connotations of savings; Medicare deals with health problems of older Americans, with an emphasis on paying someone's bills. Social Security is a pay-as-you-go program, with no direct part in increasing the deficit; Medicare, as it does affect the escalating "fee-for-service" structure of health care, is potentially part of the growing deficit. While each of these issues can be explained and justified, we are making them here to underscore the greater *political* vulnerability Medicare faces that Social Security does not. It therefore will take much more concrete effort to avoid larger cuts in the coming years.

Of course, Medicare has been solvent since its inception, bringing in more funds than it has paid out since 1973, except for a small deficit in 1977. The fund's reserve was $16.5 billion at the end of 1973 and was $18.7 billion at the end of 1981. Such reality is far different from the dire predictions initiated by the Carter and Reagan Administrations, which foresaw the fund running out of money in 1981, 1987, 1990, and 1991, respectively (New York Times, March 29, 1986). Instead, in 1986 there is a surplus of $15.7 billion, and the *Social Security Bulletin* now projects a surplus until 1998 (New York Times, March 29, 1986).

Given the quiet truth of Medicare's fiscal health that has confronted the harsh attacks against the entitlement, there has been one significant shift in Medicare itself—increasing the deductibles and copayments at each level of hospitalization. This is especially severe for both the poor and people with a long-term illness. The deductible of the first 60 days is $420—more than a 100% increase since 1980, and at least 18% of the yearly income for the minimum Social Security beneficiaries. For serious, long-term illness, however, the costs become extreme even for a middle-income individual—over $15,000 for one year's hospitalization must be borne by other income or insurance of the senior citizen. For that rapidly expanding older population—much older, more female, more isolated—these costs are especially ominous. To pay such bills for most is an impossibility. For the poor these trends have to be frightening, for the Reagan Administration's cuts in Medicaid have been far more substantial than in Medicare—over 10.1% since 1981, for a total of $18 billion (Brand, 1985: 15-17). These cuts, passed on to the states with the assumed freedom to shape their own Medicaid programs (how is one freer with less funds?), have meant marked cutbacks in the optional services such as dental care, podiatry, optometry, and prescription drugs. These are the very services that have been found particularly relevant to older people (Brand, 1985: 16), people who now go without.

These cuts are serious and have narrowed the health options of thousands of older Americans. However, such cuts left untouched the fee-for-service structure of health care that has always existed in the United States. As Paul Starr, Health-Pac, and others have documented, all the original health-insurance plans (Blue Cross and Blue Shield) left in place the payment structure of individualized doctor-patient care of the past. Instead of restructuring the expanding hospital and health services to emphasize prevention and flat-payment group plans, every fee for consultation, medicine, tests, procedures, surgery, etc. was charged at the market rate plus costs. Many ill people were victimized through overtesting and extended, needless care (Kotelchuk, 1985). It also led to inflationary costs larger than in any other area of the welfare state—costs tripled between 1965 and 1975 at a rate of 11% every year; they tripled again in nine years at a rate of 14% each year (Grey Panther Bulletin, 1985).

The attempts to cut costs between 1978 and 1983 focused on the expanding populations that used these services; especially the poor and the very old. With gloomy economic trends and equally dire demographic presentations, the political emphasis was on cutting their entitlements rather than restructuring the health-care system itself. As that did not succeed, a new approach was devised that took the focus off the "truly needy" and moved it on to the hospitals themselves. Or so it seemed. As Gertie M. and others have found out, the Medicare changes under the Social Security Act of 1981 have put older people at more health risk than they were 15 years ago.

THE INVASION OF THE DRGs

Under the amendments to that act, Medicare now pays a fixed amount for every patient, based on diagnosis. There are 471 categories of illness, known as Diagnosis-Related Groups, or DRGs. Each DRG has an assigned dollar-value—like a menu—and each patient is diagnosed at the hospital door. There is no adjustment for severity of illness; pneumonia has a set price whether the patient stays two days or two weeks. If a hospital can treat the patient for less than the set price, it keeps the extra money. But if the hospital spends too much on treatment, it must pay the additional costs. Furthermore, the developers of the DRGs excluded all socioeconomic variables that were "outside" the hospital experience, like socioeconomic status or race (Grey Panther Bulletin, 1985). Poor groups' health needs were assumed to be the same as the well off. The Reagan Administration argued that there was no "special consideration" that the poor and *the institutions* that serve them would need.

Since the DRGs were implemented, the basic care of the elderly has diminished and the "special considerations" of the poor have not gone away, with drastic results for both groups. Regarding the latter group, a study released in November 1985 by the District of Columbia Hospital Association found that overall cost per case rises dramatically as a hospital's volume of poor patients increases. After comparing 257 hospitals in five major metropolitan areas, they found that Medicare costs average $568 per case higher among hospitals with a 10% volume of Medicaid patients than were those hospitals with no Medicaid patients. When the Medicaid population was 20%, Medicare costs were $964 higher, and when 30%, $1,118 higher (Ashby, 1984). This confirmed earlier findings by an Urban Institute study, that costs were 18% higher at institutions providing a great deal of care to the poor compared to those treating few poor (Kotelchuk, 1985). Other studies have echoed these findings.

The results are obvious—private hospitals and others with smaller case loads of poor patients are "dumping" their poor at the doors of public hospitals who cannot under law refuse them (Kotelchuk, 1985). Operating under the same DRG rules, the results have been clear cut. Whereas in 1982 (the last year of the old system) public hospitals did better financially by treating Medicare patients; by 1983 they were operating in the red. (According to Kotelchuk, Medicare costs rose $1.1 million while Medicare revenues dropped $2.46 million.) Even the softening of these cash-flow problems through increased subsidies for medical education has not been sufficient to offset the increasing cost burdens that publics bear compared to private hospitals (Fergin, 1985). As of this writing, even these education subsidies are expected to be eliminated in the budget of 1987.

The problems for the elderly poor under this system have been enormous. As poor people in general are more likely to put off treatment until they are severely ill, each illness carries the likelihood of complications. "Complications" do not fit into the DRG structure. The system only reimburses for the DRG one receives upon hospitalization. As Sheryl Fergin in "Sicker and Quicker" wrote,

If a patient shows signs of harboring another disease once he is admitted, the hospital tries to treat the first disease, discharge for seven days, and readmit him with a new DRG . . . [As one doctor noted] "A woman came in for skin cancer turned out to need a pacemaker. Both problems were handled, but the doctors were told afterwards, 'that we should have put her to sleep [operated on] for

the skin cancer, then discharged her for the pacemaker.' They lost
lots of money because they could only charge for the skin cancer"
[Fergin, 1985].

These abuses are intensified for the poor but affect all Medicare
recipients in less Draconian ways. Medical abuse had become so
severe that by October 1984, the inspector general of the Department of Health and Human Services warned "the impact of this
type of abuse (premature discharges and inappropriate transfers)
on quality is so significant that its potential visibility could jeop-
ardize the integrity of the medical review process and the payment
system" (Fergin, 1985).

Older people, especially the poor, are denied treatment and
shunted back and forth within a system that increasingly—and
purposely—ignores the complexity and fullness of their medical
needs. At the same time, those workers in the medical field who are
committed to working with the elderly and poor are under increasing strain. Doctors are being pressured for immediate diagnoses
that get the highest payment at the least cost. Doctors, nurses, and
social workers receive weekly computer printouts, which contain
patient cost breakdowns and rank doctors and other service workers by cost efficiency. Those whose "Total Days In" were over the
"Expected Length of Stay" by a significant amount have been
spoken to and subtly intimidated to improve their performance.
For the social worker who also considers such nonhospital-related
issues such as housing, family supports, and income in considering
discharge feasibility, the pressures can be even greater. Finally, it
appears as if all types of professional-service workers are being
replaced in favor of DRG coders, discharge planners, and the computer DRG software itself, which ranges in cost from $75,000 to
$200,000 (Fergin, 1985). Clinical skill is diminished and replaced
by the computer code.

It is within this institutional framework, out of sight of most
Americans, that the problems of the old have become more and
more pronounced. Health-care needs are of paramount concern for
older Americans, but their genuine success in holding the line on
income losses may disguise the enveloping tensions that occur
when they are at all sick. Once ill, especially if they are poor, older
Americans face a medical system even less supportive than in the
past. And the workers within that system are less able to provide
support than ever before.

FIGHTING BACK FOR INDEPENDENT LIVING:
FROM SOCIAL SECURITY COALITIONS TO SELF-HELP

As serious and as foreboding as these medical issues are, they probably would be far worse were it not for the level of active organizing engaged in by older Americans and their allies. It is possible to argue that no other social group in the United States has the level of political organization that older Americans do. Equally important, there are a number of vital, interesting experiments in self-help developed by the elderly and their allies speaking to forms of *independent living* that others could use as well.

The political organization is remarkably high, especially around Social Security and Medicare cuts. The primary basis to independent living must be financial. Without economic security, there is little likelihood of other forms of self-help. Recognizing this, seniors not only vote; from the more traditional American Association of Retired Persons (AARP) to the militant Grey Panthers, they are *organized*. Anticut coalitions are only the most obvious forms of this activity, with national, statewide and local groups developed to keep officials aware of their needs and legislative priorities. This is why politicians consistently vote down antisocial security programs. Organization through local, state, and national coalitions means that coalition members maintain an *active memory* on each issue, using that memory to mobilize others on their behalf. Electoral promises must be followed by some legislative follow-through or these coalitions react with threats of withdrawn support that is no idle saber-rattling. There are few politicians today in office who actively support cuts in social security. Even the Gramm-Rudman budget balancing bill of 1987 exempts Social Security from its procedural ax (New York Times, February 18, 1986: A1). These coalitions are just too strong from top to bottom to permit anything else.

However, there are other coalitions in existence, developed in equally compelling if more modest form, which are active on the other important senior issues. For example, the National Coalition for Nursing Home Reform (NCNHR) began in 1975 at the American Health Care Association's annual meeting. Half-heartedly invited by the nursing-home industry's major trade association, 13 citizen groups came to a discussion on "participating management" in nursing homes. Using this one-time opportunity as a spring board, the NCNHR was launched soon after. Led by Elma Holder, the coalition grew in ways similar to other senior activist groups. They first emphasized specific reforms agreed to by the member organizations around the country, such as the Ombudsman Program in every nursing home. By 1979, they received grants to train personnel for these programs, in collaboration with local citizen groups. This work, in turn, spawned visiting programs. Each program went on to emphasize issues that helped foster resident's councils, councils that are the essence of empowerment for any client group. As Holder commented, "One of the things [NCNHR] has always thought, is that the more involvement you have of local people, the more likely that nursing homes are going to really provide good care" (The Grey Panther, April 1986: 23-24).

It is this perspective that heavily influences many senior coalitions. The coalitions have a mix of young and old professional staff and local membership that serves as the basis for developing an organizational infrastructure far more responsive and flexible than often found in other coalition formations. We don't wish to romanticize these groupings. There are elements of staff dominance and elitism to be found in these coalitions, too. But it is only relative dominance. The consistency of older Americans' quick response on every repeated attempt to cut Social Security speaks to membership vigilance and engagement that is exciting. Older Americans aren't simply large in numbers. Those numbers act in a concerted fashion that give them significant influence over the entitlements that most directly affect them.

This vigilance is borne out of more than organizations. It also stems from the conditions of ageism that old people face in the United States. Forced out of the labor market at 65 and marginalized by attitudes of fear and condescension (Crystal, 1984), older Americans have had to look to themselves first for group support in their quest to live out their lives with respect and independence. What has emerged, while not well known to others, has often been the essence of genuine empowerment. For example, Susan Perlstein's "Elders Share the Arts" in New York has joined reminiscence, cultural dialogue, and dramatic technique in developing a group work program that is artistically exciting and empowering at the same time. Such groups use an engaged process of "life review" to reflect on their lives and through that reflection to gain added strength for more engaged activism. Such groups increasingly have influence in their senior centers, even when little seemed to exist before.

More often the work in local areas has centered on self-help and the health-related self-care projects. Such projects are empowering, however, only under certain important conditions. For unlike the political coalitions around entitlement cuts, many self-help projects of the old are clearly prepolitical. As Reissman (1984) and others have written, the initial work surrounding self-help seems to flow out of a combination of immediate personal stresses and a breakdown in other social supports (especially family units) that make individuals especially vulnerable.[2] This vulnerability, be it physical illness, social isolation, or parenting needs, calls for a significant measure of immediate, concrete, supportive services, education, and feedback by professionals and other self-help group members. For example, a self-care program for older residents living near the Fair Haven (CT) Community Mental Health Clinic found that seniors were interested in self-care but were physically unable to attend many meetings. Working with senior members and professionals in service and media work, the clinic developed a closed-circuit television program for the elderly in the apartment building in which the forum met. Tapes were then made available to the community and shown at local senior centers. People then gave feedback on future programs that served as the basis for later programming. In turn, activists then noted increased interest in other, more political events.

A number of other, varied self-help groups have grown up in locales over the years.[3] MASH (Mutual Aid Self-Help) developed among older Mexican Americans as a natural helping network in organizing service volunteers. SAGE (Senior Action for a Gay Environment) began as a mutual support group for older gays and lesbians who found few traditional services available for them in terms of natural older concerns, especially the death of lovers and lifelong partners. The group has flourished into a far more expansive group over the last five years. Senior Gleaners in California is composed of low-income retired people who travel around California picking fruits and vegetables left after harvest. The 1700-member organization has gleaned over 400 tons of produce that they distributed to themselves and to 30 charities as well. In a very different setting, the Arthritis Clinic at Downstate Medical Center developed an older person's support group that began with an emphasis on physical exercise and evolved into an outside social and planning network of group members.

While all of these groups are important, the greatest number seem to be in health care, for they help older Americans in two critical areas: prevention and the care and treatment of chronic disease. By sharing information and giving support about how to follow health routines of diet, exercise, and other disease-preventive activities, these groups both improve a member's health and break down isolation that otherwise undermines the potential for ongoing engagement in other, more politicized activities.

Left by itself, this kind of self-help runs the danger of substituting for services the larger society has a responsibility to offer. Reissman and those at the National Self-Help Clearing House recognize this. Activists and professionals need to work with these self-care groups to make the connections between their daily activities and larger social/political issues. When successful, the three stages of self-help that grow to empowerment include

(1) The process of mutual help begins to develop competencies of working together and sharing, which activists point out can be applied to larger issues. As Reissman (1984: 3) says, "The beginnings of empowerment emerge as people begin to feel able to control some aspect of their lives."

(2) Advocacy can emerge as self-helpers discover the external causes of their problems. Ageism, as with other forms of oppression, leaves people with feelings of internalized blame and self-doubt. By helping people to become more aware of other sources of responsibility, activists increase people's awareness of their own condition:

> Underlying this is the basic self-help ethos that emphasizes the indigenous strengths of the people involved in contrast to a dependence on external, elite supports. These attitudes are in contrast to a lobbyist form of advocacy in which representatives speak for the constituents while the latter remain passive [Reissman, 1984: 3].

(3) Out of these prepolitical forms there may emerge a consciousness of the inner connections between self-help networks and groups and those larger anticut coalitions for political change. The National Self-Help Clearing House has identified a number of groups that suggest how clearly the "personal" and the "political" issues of older Americans are joined. Such is the nature of real empowerment.

It also seems evident that seniors seem to have had significant success at joining the personal and the political because of the proliferation of senior citizen centers that developed since the 1970s. Like many of the other groups working under the safety net, these centers are locally based, relatively decentralized, and have a high mix between member activists and professional staff. While these centers serve only 7% of the entire older population, their numbers are large enough to have significant impact on people's lives. And, of course, most centers do not *emphasize* empowering forms of self-help and political change. They have card games, recreation, dance, and staff-to-client workshops on any number of issues. But within every center and among most staffs are people who approach the blend of self-help organization and political activism in the empowering ways that Reissman spells out. They thus serve as willing troops and engaged activists in the antientitlement coalitions that have been so effective in countering conservative agendas.

This work isn't easy. But the vigilance, activism, and mutual support that many older Americans engage in are exemplars of the political-personal support strategies that effective work under the safety net demands.

APPENDIX:
Questions and Activities

Personal
— What are your feelings about old people? Do you feel they have the same skills as others younger than they are? Do you avoid them because they scare you a little in making you think of your own aging?

Programmatic
— Investigate programs in your local area. You can start with local senior centers listed in a phone book.
— Self-help programs can be found at senior centers and within other organizations like the Grey Panthers. Contact hospitals and health clinics if you wish to volunteer for health-related self-care programs.
— To start a self-help program, you need to do the following:
    (a) have older Americans identify the problem in their terms
    (b) emphasize concrete services and information in each meeting
    (c) identify skills and resources of group members themselves
— Ongoing self help groups emphasize:
    (a) mutual sharing
    (b) activities that minimize isolation of individuals

   (c) in-health settings, some physical exercise, and other pre-
       ventive techniques that members can use on their own
— Empowering self-help groups include:
   (a) information on external causes to their problems
   (b) feedback on their own strengths, skills, and improved
       capacities
   (c) clear programmatic connections between the self-help
       work and other coalition work.

Coalition Work
— Coalitions for Social Security and Medicare exist in most communities. You can find out about them by contacting people in
  senior centers, or by visiting groups like the Grey Panthers or
  the American Association of Retired Persons.
— These well-developed coalitions have campaigns to join. Activities include petitioning, fund-raising, and lobbying. Have your
  group members engage in the tactics of greatest interest to them.
  Speakers from the coalitions can be invited if members wish.
— Have the group select representatives to attend the coalition on
  a consistent basis.

NOTES

   1. Myers (1981) compares U.S. rates and levels of state pension plans with
those in Europe (pp. 26-27).
   2. *Social Policy,* under the leadership of Frank Reissman and others at the
National Self-Help Clearing House, has written consistently on the progressive
dimension to self-help since 1983. The journal is a valuable resource for those
interested in self-help.
   3. See "Self-Help and the Elderly," *Social Policy* (January/February 1984).
SAGE is not discussed by the journal but is well known in New York and other
metropolitan areas.

Chapter 5

BLACK, SINGLE-PARENT WOMEN

There is nothing worse in the United States than a welfare cheat. Except for the most violent criminals, the images surrounding welfare recipients are some of the most unrelentingly hostile in American life: lazy, shiftless, addictive, unwilling to work, sexually promiscuous. It's a long list, one that has been used in our history to intimidate and discourage as many people as possible from joining its rolls. Now, in the 1980s there has been an updated description added to an already long list—dependent—the dependent welfare client, the individual caught "in a cycle of dependency," whose behavior evolved in great response to the nature of the *welfare state itself*. The new term is important, for it speaks to a different focus for the blame: the welfare system. Implicit in this modern focus is another most unmodern objective: the dismantling of welfare and its related services.

The argument seems obvious. Before you can break the cycle of dependency, you must break the cause of the dependency in the first place. This cycle, so the argument goes, has created a whole new population of individuals *no longer capable* of the independent, striving behavior and values necessary to work well and hard in the increasingly competitive and demanding private sector. The dependent lifestyle is so normless and dependent on shifts in welfare benefits that most welfare families' behaviors are fit to them. Teenage pregnancy, single-parent families, and unethical behavior ("getting over") are all seen as a response to this welfare-induced cycle. Without drastic changes in the welfare system, the argument continues, there can be no changes in such self-destructive behaviors.

These arguments echo earlier theories of behavior related to the poor, especially the "culture of poverty" theories.[1] But these latter theories rarely identified the problem in terms of *government intervention;* in fact, most stressed the need for public aid and services to counter the negative effects within these "poor cultures." Today's cycle of dependency theorists, led most notably by Charles Murray (1982) and George Gilder (1980), see the problem in the intervention itself. Such arguments have forced social service workers everywhere into an extremely defensive posture. The problems seem so complex, and given the apparently trenchant statistical evidence of Murray[2] (more on that later), policymakers and practitioners alike have seemed incapable of marshaling either solid evidence or strong counterarguments to stem the conservative tide of antiwelfare state ideology. After all, how does one respond to descriptions such as the following:

> They have taken a practical attitude toward sex and quite unashamedly behave as nature guides them. The illegitimate child . . . was never viewed with the disdain awarded unfortunates in other societies . . . Illegitimates make up a sizable percentage of the population, and, though the circumstances of their birth sometimes called for off-color jokes, they were not severely rejected or scorned.

> The new unwed mothers promptly appear(ed) at the welfare offices and applied for their monthly assistance checks. In due course, the first 'mistake' was followed by another and the monthly stipend grew . . . These 'welfare mothers' thus support their children and themselves and sometimes assist their parents as well [Caudill, 1963: 286-287; see also Leoff, 1971].

Everybody knows whom the above is describing—the rising "underclass" whose misery is intensified and expanded by the "feminization of poverty" as well. The solutions to those two complicated social issues seem so great that many people understandably are drawn to Murray's work. Perhaps hard work and the strengthening lash of free-market forces might make the difference in slackening amoral behavior and dependency—except for one not-so-minor problem. The above quotation comes not from our urban-minority underclass, but from Appalachian white poor. Written in about the 1960s, such descriptions included lurid and often moralistic renderings of the white poor's behavior, which included acts of promiscuity, drunkenness, beatings, and other clinically pathological diagnoses (Caudill, 1963). However, stripped of the political explosiveness of gender and race common to today's discussions, these very real behavioral and moral problems were always analyzed *within the context* of multigenerational unemployment, chronic joblessness, and regional dynamics. Likewise, solutions emphasized an economic and social "Marshall Plan" for Appalachia; an "Appalachian Valley Authority" similar to the TVA; massive economic development that could generate jobs and income security before or in conjunction with other, more clinically based services (Caudill, 1963).

Such solutions neither denied nor ignored the real individual pathology, forms of addiction, and violence that occurred within this group. But *these issues were seen as impossible to solve if the economic context was not altered first*. It is a mark of the *political* direction of our times that once clearly identified symptoms of economic distress are once again being reified into primary factors of causality. Like the Social Darwinists of a century ago, who rooted one's economic failure within an individual's character, today's conservatives (and, all too often, well-meaning progressives) see solutions in highly personalized terms. At best, they have given the argument of individualized responsibility a new twist by emphasizing collective responsibility of a particular *social group* to help end the downward spiral of hopelessness. This seems most evident when speaking of the poor black family, where both conservative black leaders like Glenn Lowry (1986) and progressives like Jesse Jackson are increasing their own calls for the *black community itself* to stem the tide of amoral, dependent behaviors they see.[3]

As this chapter will argue, there are enough data to suggest that the fundamental problem currently facing single-parent families lies less in complexity than in the obfuscations surrounding the conditions under which poor, single, and disproportionately minority mothers live. We will make this argument by addressing the issues and currently popular solutions that concern the single-parent family today. In particular, we will assess the degree to which the "feminization of poverty" affects these families; the amount of dependency created within poor families, especially poor black families; and the viability of both voluntaristic self-help programs and public-funded, "jobs training/job-creating" programs, especially the once-popular WIN (Work Incentive) program and the currently fashionable workfare program.

Having this broader policy and programmatic discussion suggests immediately that the level of successful service intervention and advocacy is at a much more preliminary stage than we see in other areas of service under the safety net. Unlike work with the disabled, there is no clear organizational focus such as the Independent Living Centers that are discussed in Chapter 6. Nor is there as broad a consensus on the rights of this group to widespread entitlements as there has been for seniors as we discuss in Chapter 4. For those who are impatient with policy discussion and anxious to help, this chapter will serve as a tactical reminder that until one is sufficiently clear on the "definition of the problem" to mobilize concerted efforts toward "problem resolution," there is not much one can do effectively. We must not confuse our commitment to social injustice with strategic or programmatic effectiveness. Right now there is little being done effectively to help single-parent families because of so little agreement on what is really wrong and why the problems of single-parent families seem so complex.

Given the inability of progressives to marshall a concerted counterattack to the conservative agenda, the Reagan Administration, with the bilateral support of Congress, utilized the Omnibus Reconciliation Act (OBRA) of 1981 to cut drastically benefits for Aid to Families with Dependent Children (AFDC). By instituting a series of five administrative changes in determining levels of eligibility, allowable expenses, and client earnings (Joe and Rogers, 1986: chap. 3), case loads dropped between 10% and 13.7% between 1982 and 1985, with an overall reduction in costs of 14.3% (p. 95). Most of the 370,000 to 507,000 families removed were working poor. Such figures indicate that without a concerted effort to redefine the problems faced by these poor families, their conditions will get worse.

THE FEMINIZATION OF POVERTY AND ITS MEANING FOR SINGLE-PARENT FAMILIES

Lacking clarity, we need first to investigate policy issues in terms of their *social dimensions* so that we can ascertain whether or not patterns of employment, poverty, education, and the like can be explained by individualized phenomena alone. If, for example, there were the same percentages of poor women as poor men in single-parent households in various age categories, we could say there was no need to factor gender into our programmatic responses to help ameliorate single-parent family problems. However, if there are significant differences, then programs would have to differentiate and intensify their services for the more disadvantaged populations. The former pattern is preferred by conservatives because it roots problems on a more individualized basis and finds less fault in the organization of present social/economic relationships. For progressives, the latter pattern suggests societywide constraints and inequalities that any program must address as well. (Needless to say, the latter is also more expensive in short-term programmatic costs.)

A quick review of Bureau of Census Data reveals profound shifts in single-parent families between 1970 and 1982—a 49% increase for men and 105% increase for women. That's more than a twofold increase for women over men. These households are disproportionately poor—women head over half of all poor families and over half the children of female-headed households are poor; 50% of white children and 68% of black and Hispanic children (Stallard et al., 1983: 14). So clear is the spiraling pattern of women's impoverishment that the President's National Advisory Council on Economic Opportunity in 1981 wrote,

> All others being equal, if the proportion of female-headed household's families were to continue to increase at the same rate it did from 1967 to 1978, the poverty population would be composed solely of women and their children before the year 2000 [Stallard et al., 1983: 14].

To frame that quotation in terms of inequality, the median income of a female household head, no husband present, was $10,408; for black women it was $7,245 and for Hispanic women it was $7,031. Men in equivalent positions made over $17,000 annually (U.S. Bureau of the Census, 1981). Equivalent studies in 1985 show no proportionate change (New York Times, February 12, 1985).

These figures speak to a more societywide form of discrimination than can be accounted for by simple individual preference or predisposition. Equally important in terms of our discussion here, it becomes evident that women must work longer hours to make the equivalent wages of men. For further data show that the occupations in which women are placed are as "segregated as they were at the end of the Victorian era" (Pearce, 1978). "Women are systematically paid less than men in equivalent positions. Even when men and women share the *same* occupations, men's earnings are far larger than women's. Full-time female clerical workers averaged $9,855 in 1981 while men in the same position average $16,503" (Stallard et al., 1983: 9). This discriminatory pattern holds true all the way up the income scale. Less than 2% of all female workers earned $25,000 or more in 1981, compared to 17.5% of all men.

These statistics reveal a pattern of systemwide discrimination and inequality that *structurally impedes* the job entry, career mobility, and financial independence of women. Even if one ignores other issues like child care or sexual harassment on the job, these structural impediments carry with them narrowed options and fewer choices for women who work. Women work—in 1985, 52% of all women did so—but the positive connotations of self-actualization, mobility, and independence that "work" suggests to some does not hold for the vast majority of women in the workplace.

CHILD CARE

The problem of economic inequality is large enough. However, as women continue to perform the preeminent tasks of childcare,[4] there is an added dimension to the feminization of poverty that intensifies the difficulties that women, especially single-parent women, face in escaping poverty and the need for welfare. For even if employed full time, women face unyielding child-care demands. There are no industrywide programs to support women who work or who are looking for work, and the few public programs, such as the Massachusetts job-training program, limit child care to the initial period of training at worksites (New York Times, November 18, 1985). As almost half of all single women with children under 6, and two-thirds of those with children between 6 and 17, were in the labor force, child-care demands must be intense and solutions problematic. Only 15% of all preschool children were enrolled in licensed child-care services in 1980; since then, services have been halved by cuts in federal and state subsidies. Thus, while economic insecurity is driving more and more women into an already discriminatory job market, fiscal cuts in child-care programs are marginalizing more and more poor women in their attempts to attain meaningful employment.

We cannot sidestep the importance of these findings. If such rates were to continue into the year 2000, the majority of white families and 80% of all black families would be headed by single parents.

These trends cry out for solution because they create the potential for social havoc—increased crime, drugs, illiteracy, prostitution. Today's more popular solutions suggest that these trends and the havoc they induce emerge out of a combination of welfare dependency, family pathology, and social disorganization. Having ignored the gender-based structural impediments discussed above, today's "welfare dependency" theorists focus on the poor black women and their families who receive AFDC and other entitlements. To theorists like Charles Murray (1982), the poor's problems flow from liberalized rules of the welfare state that foster dependency and undermine self-respect and self-reliance. Murray (p. 9) writes,

> The most compelling explanation for the marked shift in the fortunes of the poor is that they continue to respond, as they always had, to the world as they found it, but that we—meaning the not poor and the undisadvantaged—had changed the rules of their world . . . The first effect of the new rules was to make it profitable for the poor to behave in the short-term in ways that were destructive in the long-term. Their second effect was to mask these long-term losses—to subsidize irretrievable mistakes.

He concludes with calls for workfare instead of welfare, economic self-reliance instead of welfare-state dependency, and moral/social reeducation through self-help and voluntary religious/civic organizations instead of publically subsidized job-training programs. Lest one think social-science writing is devoid of political consequences, compare Murray's previous statement with Ronald Reagan's critique of the welfare state as he called for a "major overhaul" of the welfare system:

> In 1964, the famous War on Poverty was declared and a funny thing happened. Poverty, as measured by dependency, stopped shrinking and then actually began to grow worse. I guess you could say poverty won the war . . . And this is why I am calling once again on the American people to do away with those programs that sap initiative and undermine our social fabric. [New York Times, February 23, 1986].

THE ASSUMPTIONS OF DEPENDENCY AMONG POOR BLACK WOMEN: MYTH VERSUS REALITY, PART 1

Of course, there are problems to be found among poor women and their families, including poor black women. The alarming percentages of poor black women heading households with children frightens everyone. A majority of black children born in 1986 are poor, and likely to remain so (Holmes Norton, 1985). Murray argues that the explosion of the welfare roles in the 1960s, caused by the spread of universal entitlements under the Great Society Programs of Lyndon Johnson, has greatly fostered this trend by allowing these women to receive easily hefty, monthly welfare checks, food stamps, and other allowances for each child born. Why work when you can do so well on the dole?

Given the economic discrimination women face in the job market, one could understand Murray's argument. (Murray does not discuss racial and gender-based dynamics in the private sector, but assumes they are benign.[5]) The actual findings on poor black women and work belie any possibility of reliance on welfare grants. Census data analyzed by Bette Woody and Micheline Maison reveal that the mean *annual AFDC payments of all black women heading households averaged $550.59 in families with children 18 years of age and younger.*[6] For single black women with children under five, the grants *drop* to $394.86 a year. (Equivalent white women receive $660.57 and $758.67, respectively. While low absolute figures, both signify important racial differences in how black women are treated on welfare, especially since the white families had fewer children; Woody and Maison, 1985: 28-29.) On a monthly basis, all these figures break down to a range of $32.85 to $63.22 a month—hardly enough for anyone to live on. While these national data are mean averages, with some families receiving nothing and others the maximum of $5,028, the stark reality to this pattern is obvious. Few women, *especially poor black women with very young children,* received such large annual allotments from welfare as to stay above the poverty line, let alone afford ease and comfort. A ten-year panel study headed by Duncan (1985) at the University of Michigan suggests similar findings, indicating that the low grants are based on people's intermittent use of AFDC. Only 8.3% of all women received welfare for five or more years; 4.4% for eight years or more. Poor black women with children don't receive large welfare grants. That's reality number one.

MYTH VERSUS REALITY, PART 2

The second myth relates to the assumption that poor black women do not work. Census data for 1982 indicate that the majority of *all* black women are in the labor force (i.e., working or actively seeking work). Forty-eight percent of poor women with children under six years of age are employed; 60.9% of those with children between 6-18 years are working (Woody and Maison, 1985: 29). Furthermore, while the number of hours a mother worked per week was influenced by the presence and ages of children for white women, this is not true for black women. Black women heading families are more likely to work when they must care for young children. *In fact, working black women who have children under five years of age worked more hours of work per week than any other category of female householders—37.3 hours a week.* The next highest hours were held by black women with children under 18 (34.2 hours); followed by white women who headed households with no spouse present (32.3) (adapted from Hayghe, 1982).

We have dwelled on these statistics, drawn from the federal *Monthly Labor Review,* because they are so at odds with the popular myths about poor, single black mothers. *Just as they receive the least aid from AFDC, those in the labor force work more hours than any other group of women.* The welfare allotment does not seem to create dependency. The data indicate that women work long and hard. Furthermore, they have child-care responsibilities equal to or greater than any other group. While there may be more women receiving the small annual welfare allotments (which helps explain why total expenditures have risen), the actual average amount these women receive means a long, hard existence for daily survival that is neither caused nor intensified by welfare dependency.

Initiative can be seen in terms of educational achievement as well. Most black women with children under 18 years of age have completed at least high school: 41.2% have 12 years of schooling, while another 15% have completed 1-3 years of college. These percentages increase for older women, suggesting that their interest in self-improvement is not exhausxted at an early age (Woody and Maison, 1985: 27).

THE LONG-TERM WELFARE POOR:
MYTH VERSUS REALITY, PART 3

But wait a second. If there are all these hard-working, struggling people, what about the very real social problems of increased teenage pregnancy, drug addiction, violent crime? Those figures are real, and *somebody* must be doing something wrong. Let's not use statistics, as so many have, to blur reality! Perhaps that 8.3% is a relatively small proportion of all welfare recipients. But isn't that number large enough in absolute terms—a few million people—to make a significant difference on the quality of life in white and black communities?

Before turning to look more carefully at this poorest group, it's important to detour just a little and correct Murray's—and others'—perceptions about some areas of pathology and deviance. If the dependency theorists are right, issues like crime and teenage pregnancy should have skyrocketed for poor blacks after 1965, when the looser eligibility requirements were created through the Great Society. However, Irving Piliavin (1985: 60-62) points out that the relative increase of nonwhite arrest rates was much less than that of whites:

> Overall, between 1960 and 1980 the relative increase in white arrest rates was 30% higher than of non-whites for property crimes and more than 300% higher than of nonwhites for violent crimes.

Murray has argued that it is inappropriate to compare rates of these two groups because black's baseline of crime was so much higher in 1960. One could also make this argument when comparing present teenage pregnancy rates. As Joyce Ladner (1986) has documented, the explosive rate in teen pregnancy is among young, white women, while the rate for black teenagers is actually dropping.

As these data suggest, the phenomenon is societywide, not racially segregated. For our discussion here, however, these statistics underline the point that the social problems faced by poor blacks were in place *before* the Great Society programs were ever conceived of, let alone implemented. Likewise, whites are facing these problems in recent years, when the impact of the Great Society was diminishing. Taking these varying trends together—one with a high baseline before the Great Society, the other increasing after its impact had decreased—we can suggest that the problems each group confronts are rooted less within the welfare state than within an economic structure that creates long-term poverty for blacks and escalating poverty for whites. In 1948, 87% of all black men were part of the labor force, one percentage point higher than white males. In 1960, the percentages were the same for white men, while 74% of black men were in the labor force. The 1950s ushered in the period of long-term unemployment for blacks and is the time during which black rates of crime grew sharply. White males' rates of employment dropped in the 1970s. This is the period in which the explosive rates of crime Piliavin reported grew most rapidly (Piliavin, 1985; Danziger and Gottschalk, 1985). High crime rates and large numbers of births among young women always have been associated with the poor in almost every country in the world. While not fashionable today, this enduring truth brings us back to focus on other problems within society, ones that do not assume the economic system is as benign and self-enhancing as Murray (1982) implies (see his final chapter in particular).

We will return to these larger systemic issues later. Now it is important to look at the poorest of the black community, for it is they that Murray and Gilder focus upon in their descriptive renderings of how the poor avoid work and create pathology. After all, many argue, it is not as if crime, family disorganization, illiteracy, and high levels of unwanted births are not happening. They are. Perhaps there's something special about this population—be it 8% or 4%—that needs to be dealt with more forcefully.

Until recently, there had been little that systematically looked at this population in a manner allowing for reliable generalizations. While works like Liebow's *Talley's Corner* (1957) had powerful conceptual power, such studies were based on too small a sample or showed other forms of sampling error so as to limit the empirical impact of their conclusions. Fortunately, Leonard Goodwin's (1985) work goes a long way toward correcting this limited data base. He systematically examined 1400 WIN (Work Incentive Program) recipients in two cities between 1978 and 1980, using a comparison group of unemployment insurance recipients. His work encompassed both poor black men and women, their attitudes about work and welfare, whether or not such attitudes changed over time, and their experiences with both welfare and work (Goodwin, 1985: 15-17).

He found that, like most Americans, few men or women preferred welfare to work. Most found it humiliating and burdensome to receive welfare. Such results are not that surprising, being consonant with what most Americans believe. What is illuminating, however, are the social psychological effects of long-term unemployment on the poor. "Bad attitudes" toward work (not seeing it as valuable, worth doing, etc.) evolved among men *after* the frustrations associated with not getting a long-term job, losing jobs again and again, or only attaining access to low-wage, dead-end jobs.

Only as the experience of work (or the lack of it) was frustrating did men alter their ideas about the value of work. Furthermore, increased marital disruption occurred not *after* poor men accepted welfare but during the frustrating period surrounding their desire to work and their inability to do so (Goodwin, 1985: 81-107). Marriage tensions arose not *with* welfare but from the thought of being on welfare, the stigmatization, and the inability to locate meaningful, adequately paying jobs. Indeed, Goodwin's (pp. 100-103) group of welfare fathers were less willing to stay on welfare when job opportunities arose than were a comparison group of fathers receiving unemployment insurance.

Only those few married fathers who accepted welfare over work were able to avoid this disruption. Goodwin traced these attitudes to a shift in one's social-psychological definition of self-worth. *Only after repeated frustrations with the job market did these men, in a search for continued self-esteem, shift away from perceptions of work as a measure of success.* To have held on to the idea that work was valuable meant continuing losses of self-worth that were too intolerable.

As Goodwin noted, like Liebow before him, this conscious shift in attitudes regarding work and self-worth did not mean an end to problematic behavior. Society's messages over what and who is and is not valued do not leave one simply through an act of will, especially when one is bombarded with commercial images of material success on a daily basis through popular media. Violence, crime, addiction, and unstable relationships were prevalent among such men, and women often had to live with the brutality caused by drunken rage or through random street-corner violence. Gilder and others see these behaviors as caused by the "ghetto scene." In contrast, Goodwin understatedly concludes,

> Conservatives fail to understand the importance that many poor men attach to supporting their families and the process by which they may throw in the towel on that issue because of lack of opportunity for training and jobs [Goodwin, 1985: 98].

PROGRAMMATIC ALTERNATIVES
FOR POOR BLACK FAMILIES:
DIFFERENT REALITIES, DIFFERENT MYTHS

As innumerable black commentators have pointed out, the above economic scenario for poor black men ties their experience closely to that of black women. One group cannot be discussed without looking at the other. Poverty, not a search for welfare payments, haunts them both. But programmatically most recent welfare-related employment projects have focused on black women. This seems due to their ongoing child-care responsibilities, their higher level of poverty and the increasing problems faced by their households. Seeing such socially complex problems looming in the very immediate future, many wish to intervene with services to stem the social onslaught these families face.

However, if a careful review of economic realities should give conservative pause before it redirects policy, then progressives must give pause when we review programmatic history. Goodwin develops a thoughtful review of some of the most prominent job-training, job-creating programs. The Welfare Demonstration Project (WDP) created 5,000 jobs for AFDC recipients in 12 sites across four states during 1972-1974 (Goodwin, 1985: 5). These generally clerical and service jobs were meaningful positions, often with union affiliation, and recipients received regular paychecks from the agencies, not from the welfare office.

Ongoing evaluation found 80% of the supervisors rating the AFDC mothers at least as efficient and willing to learn as regular employees. Ninety percent of the participants reported an increased feeling of confidence about obtaining and holding permanent jobs.

But the WDP jobs were not permanent. After two years the jobs were terminated. Goodwin dryly summarized the study's conclusions:

> Termination of the public employment experiment left welfare participants about where they started: many of them unable to find jobs at which they could support their families, and those who were employed getting the same wages (as non-participants). The fact that these welfare recipients did flow into the subsidized jobs when they were available and did carry them out effectively, however, substantiates our view that labor-market limitations are a major cause of the welfare problem [Goodwin, 1985: 136].

Another large-scale job program was the 1973 Work Relief Employment Project (WREP), which assigned 14,000 New York City home-relief recipients (mostly males) to public-sector jobs. Interviews showed the WREP workers were as productive as other workers, above average in willingness to learn and ability to get along with coworkers. WREP workers reported similar satisfactions reported above with WDP participants. Unfortunately, the same results regarding permanent employment occurred as well—only 25% were able to move into the regular work force.

A major, countrywide experiment involving 1600 randomly assigned AFDC mothers took place in 1976. The objective of this effort was to provide these mothers with a supported work situation involving job training and hands-on work experience. A comparison group of AFDC mothers not included in the experiment also were involved in the study. At the study's inception 95% of the supported group and 14.5% of the latter group were working. At the end of the experiment, when support had stopped, the difference had shrunk to 7%.

As Goodwin wrote: "A familiar pattern appears: welfare persons are able to perform well in subsidized jobs but many of them cannot make the transition to the regular work force . . . Training welfare mothers for low-skilled jobs, even under the best of conditions, cannot resolve the welfare problem unless there is a concomitant effort to raise wages and increase the number of these jobs" (Goodwin, 1985: 137).[7]

WORKFARE

And then there is workfare, the presumably new policy of "work for welfare" enunciated by Ronald Reagan and embraced by well-known liberals like Mario Cuomo of New York (Village Voice, 1985: 3). However, the newness of this program is as questionable as its effectiveness. Cardinal Richelieu, Goodwin pointed out, in 1625 called for the creation of institutions "in all cities of our realm" where "able-bodied poor could be employed in public works." In 1789, Alexander Hamilton organized the New York Manufacturing Society for the purpose of having people work in exchange for public assistance. By 1820, the effort proved economically unfeasible and collapsed, being unable to lower welfare rolls and costs.

Ignoring history, today's political leaders prefer to list three equally invalid empirical assertions as to why workfare is needed: (1) workfare will discourage malingerers; (2) improve participants' job skills and work habits, thus helping them achieve economic independence; and (3) provide useful community work in return for welfare payments.

Every systematic study reported here—and others performed as far back as 1961 (U.S. Department of Health, Education and Welfare, 1962)—refutes these assertions. Evidence collected in

California during Reagan-initiated workfare (in 1973-1974) show further evidence of failure. There was no decline in county welfare rolls that utilized workfare as compared to those where it was absent (Employment Department of California, 1978). All studies show no skill development, no heightened employability; at best, people found make-work to do. Recent studies suggest that all of these problems were intensified for women with children, for there were no workfare provisions for children.

This unending litany of programmatic failure reflected in all work-related job programs for welfare recipients must therefore be analyzed within the overall economic context. When supported with a modicum of training, income, and supervision, participants responded well. There is nothing in the empirical literature that shows a sizable pool of welfare malingerers in these programs. But the outcomes were always the same—subsidized programs provided no more jobs for participants than could have been found independently. While a few very small and specifically targeted, subsidized programs did provide some training, the most common form of skill development related to "job readiness," a level of training dooming its participants to dead-end jobs.

IMPLICATIONS FOR THE FUTURE:
UNDOING MYTHS, FOSTERING REALITIES
THAT CREATE CHANGE

Workfare has been counterproductive. WIN found jobs for 9% of WIN mothers and 18% of WIN fathers. Other targeted programs like WREP had insignificant increases in participant employability. *The economic outcome for participants left them where they were before, and the social-psychological impact must be devastating. Such welfare programs do not foster dependency; they perpetuate dishonesty.* No job-training program used any of its resources to explore, even briefly, an awareness of labor-market history that could practically prepare participants for the job market they face. Done carefully, such an examination helps externalize the source of members' problems so that further social-psychological damage is not done. Instead, by ignoring history and simply holding out the promise of job enhancement, these programs intensified more induced feelings of helplessness and hopelessness among its participants. As one welfare advocate in New York bitterly put it:

"Getting over?" I'll tell you who "gets over" on these jobs programs—the people running them who promise people everything
and deliver next to nothing. People (the participants) get their hopes
up, they try, and then a year later they're left out to dry. The people
who've got the nice jobs are the trainers, not the trainees . . . and
then you wonder why people figure why not rip off a little (on welfare) or run some scam? [interview, Feb. 18, 1986].

Of course, it is not human-services workers' fault if they cannot
find jobs that don't exist. Such issues are part of larger economic
and social forces that small groups cannot effect alone without the
support of wide-scale social movements. No one is asking them to
lose their jobs as a vehicle to create such movements by simply
criticizing the economic system. But human-service workers who
work in such programs do have the responsibility to confront honestly job-market realities as part of the context for ongoing skill
development so that fostered illusions don't later turn to internalized self-blame. One needs to foster a "critical consciousness," as
Freire (1962) puts it,[8] by interweaving a mix of imposed external
conditions and internally developed opportunities.

Analyzing economic realities while simultaneously creating
and demanding skill development from participants will prepare
them to act on the world with far greater clarity than they could in
the past. To deal realistically with one's options may be initially
painful for trainer and trainee alike, but, *as part of an active skill-
development process,* such a message carries with it the liberating,
externalized vision that locates primary responsibility where it
belongs. On the one hand, economic institutions (both private sector and public sector) must create enough jobs for everyone. On the
other hand, participants must have the skills to perform those jobs
when and if they become available. By not fostering illusions about
either the harshness of economic life or the real effort it takes to
achieve marketable skills, human-service workers can honestly
provide needed services of real value for recipients.

To ignore larger economic conditions because of their harshness
while minimizing the demands associated with real job skills is to
trivialize and demean the client. One's motives may be consciously
benign, but the continued abuse, internalized blame, and failure
that help foster pathology will only be intensified. Perhaps if we
become more modest in what we promise, we can accomplish
more.

It is important that concerned service workers, advocates, and community groups frame this problem carefully, for the underlying problem that surfaces again and again is not pathology but jobs, not welfare dependency but lack of economic independence. The multigenerational impact of joblessness and underemployment, as reflected in the structural inequalities discussed in this chapter's first section, is devastating. It has been just as devastating on Appalachian whites, whose problems, it is agreed, must be dealt with in regional and economic terms. Perhaps the combination of racial composition and geographic isolation makes it easier to root the causality of their personal behavior more in economic than social terms. After all, there are few young, white Appalachian members of the "underclass" riding the subways every day. They instead perform their violence, alcohol and drug abuse, and crime in far-off mountains, the distance of which perhaps enables policymakers to use history, economic trends, and social realities clearly as they pose realistic explanations and solutions to pathological behavior.

With so much popular talk of welfare dependency and its associated pathologies, there is a lot less clarity surrounding solutions to problems within poor black households. We have tried to answer most conservative arguments in this chapter. But there is another, well-meaning, but potentially dangerous tendency that we have noted emanating from progressive sectors as well. In particular, some black leaders like Jesse Jackson and moderate scholars like Glenn Lowry have taken a position of "moral responsibility to one's own." In their willingness to assume the "mantle of leadership [needed] to end once and for all the oppressive conditions of our people" (as Jackson said on the CBS *Bill Moyers Report* in February 1986), they suggest that black initiative, will power, and effort alone will alter substantially the abject conditions found by poor black children and their parents. A simultaneous accounting of the economic system at large is ignored, thus suggesting that black people's rededication to work, excellence, and moral uplift will be adequate (Ladner, 1986: 69).[9]

The studies reported on in this chapter make clear that if it were a matter of will power, effort, and desire there would be very, very few poor black people today. It isn't.

A more realistic way to approach the very important need to perform remedial and preventive services has been covered by Holmes Norton (1985: 93) who wrote:

[Black leaders] . . . cannot redesign the welfare system by themselves . . . [but they] are in a position to experiment with model
projects that could lead to more workable programs—such as sup-
plementing welfare grants with training or work opportunities for
single mothers; promoting family responsibility and pregnancy prevention for boys and girls through local institutions, and encourag-
ing the completion of school for single, teenaged parents.

The new black middle class, a product of the same period that saw
the weakening of the black family, still has roots in the ghetto through
relatives and friends. From churches, Girl Scout troops and settlement houses to civil rights organizations, Boys' Clubs and athletic
teams, the work of family reinforcement can be shared widely. The
possibilities for creative community intervention are many.

Such tasks are large enough and important enough without expec-
ting to accomplish more through volunteer, self-help efforts. The
black middle class are not by themselves going to create meaningful, well-paying jobs for a few million people. That will come about
only as large-scale social movements with a *very different* "definition of the problem" begin to emerge. As we discuss in the first
chapter, that problem definition must look directly at the structural
inequalities of capitalism itself. To say that, of course, is to create
nervous twists and turns among some, but what other conclusions are we left with? If we can reject the simplistic, demeaning,
and blaming assumptions of conservative forces, find patterns of
discrimination based on gender and race, and locate multigenerational unemployment among a desperate population of increasingly poor minorities, then we harm our future effectiveness by
blurring the primary locus of those problems. Indeed, the void in
our analysis will—and has been—filled by those with far more per-
nicious objectives in mind.

Even as thoughtful and rigorous a social scientist as Goodwin
and as courageous and brilliant a thinker as Holmes Norton blur
these systemic conclusions by making vague calls for "further
policy study" or "consciousness raising." Both are needed, but
toward what ends regarding the poor? Isn't there enough evidence
available to help remove the labels of blame and dependency the
poor are burdened with now as they seek to understand the problems they face?

If the trends we noted in Chapter 1 are accurate, the deindustrialization caused by capital flight is recreating a more stratified labor
force. The labor force has a narrow ribbon of extremely well-paid

workers at the top, a huge pool of unskilled, underemployed workers at the bottom. Those processes are more important in furthering the expansion of poor single-parent families than any other factor. If changed, they could significantly alter the opportunities poor children now face. The need for skills, for clear role models in parenting, education, and social behavior are still real. Human-service workers and others should work on them now and in the future. But if such remediation is not tied to a clear assessment and conscious understanding of the economic source of the most significant problems faced by single-parent families, then we must accept responsibility for perpetuating the very problems we wish to end.

As the experiences described throughout this book suggest, active processes of social change must be tied to ideas and analyses which gibe with the experiences of the people seeking that change. It may be initially intimidating to present such an analysis during such conservative and defensive times. But if we are not willing to speak to this reality, then we must be prepared to live with myths that yearly are robbing more and more American children of the chance for any future at all.

APPENDIX:
Guide Questions

Because actual service interventions need to be rethought and redeveloped more clearly for single-parent families, these questions are designed to stimulate individual and group thinking around ideas surrounding eventual program development. They can, of course, be utilized with already existing programs similar to WIN, teen pregnancy, etc.

Personal
   —What do you really *feel* when someone mentions a welfare recipient? What characteristics come to mind regarding their behavior?
   —When you find welfare clients passive and indifferent to your program, how do you react? Do you blame them or is there a more mixed response of some blame, some understanding of their plight? Or do you tend to forgive them for all their mistakes because conditions are so bad?

—How do you respond to others when they ridicule welfare clients? Do you know empirical data well enough to undermine their arguments, or do you just get angry?

Programmatic
  —What is the mix of learning about economic conditions and emphasizing specific skills for participants in your program?
  —Is the staff trained to relate larger economic and social realities in a clear way that will not overwhelm clients?
  —Are staff trained to work on the gender, racial, and class issues that differentiate the problem with different client groups?

Policy Formation/Advocacy/Organizing
  —Is your advocacy kept at an individual-case level? When do you or your group increase your advocacy to larger levels?
  —Does your programmatic formulation for a specific target group address consistently a new definition of the problem? Or does it continue to emphasize conditions at a behavioral level?
  —What other groups in your community are working on a similar "problem definition" so that you might join in coalition?
  —What mix between "self-help" and "societal responsibility" does your group have in its policy statements and suggested solutions?
  —Is there a mix of child-care, training, and economic revitalization issues developed in your work? Are the complex personal and economic demands faced by women interwoven effectively?

NOTES

1. Lewis (1965) is perhaps the best known presentation of this theory. See also Lewis (1959).

2. Murray's work purports to examine rates of increasing poverty among black Americans and the increased entitlement expenditures on welfare between 1950-1980.

3. Lowry (1986). Jackson's position is more contradicting, at times suggesting an emphasis on self-help as primary, as when he spoke on the Bill Moyers Report (February 1986), at times demanding a larger governmental role. See Harper's Magazine (1986).

4. This is true regardless of race, class, or ethnic group. For ongoing information on child-care issues of a national basis, see the newsletter Child Care, Inc., established in New York City.

5. Murray's work, rather than a reasoned empirical study, is filled with unsubstantiated assertions such as the following. Writing in his last chapter, "Choosing a Future," he imagines what would happen to adolescents "freed" from welfare's fetters. "Adolescents who were not job-ready find they are job-ready after all. It turns out that they can work for low wages and accept the discipline of the workplace if the alternative is grim enough. After a few years, many—not all, but many—find that they have acquired salable skills, or that they were at the right place at the right time, or otherwise find that the original entry-level job has gradually transformed into a secure job paying a decent wage. A few—not a lot, but a few—find that the process leads to affluence" (pp. 228-229). This mythic wonderland is not based on the economic, empirical realities touched on in the first sections of this chapter.

6. These data are so startling that certain points need to be underscored. First, this figure is for *all black women who head households*. Some may be professional women who have never been on welfare. Others may be part of the 8.3% who have been on welfare five years or more. We say that to underscore *empirical definitional issues*. However, in terms of *cultural connotation* (myth), it is this social group— "the black matriarch"—who is *assumed* to be on welfare. Clearly, economic reality and cultural myth are very different.

7. Another possibility would be to train welfare mothers for higher-level jobs. Preliminary results from a small experiment to train WIN mothers as electronics technicians reveal that some of the most skilled mothers can complete a rigorous 8-month course and obtain high paying jobs (White et al., 1981: 30). But WIN rarely provided such training and few private sector firms have committed even small resources to such an undertaking.

8. Freire (1971) is an explication of a brilliant methodology for working with the oppressed. For application of this work to the American scene, see Steve Burghardt (1982).

9. This disquieting tendency to overstate or overemphasize what the black community alone can do to solve problems confronting poor single-headed households is part of a simmering and often painful debate surrounding the Moynihan Report of 1965. This report analyzed the problems emerging in poor black families as caused primarily by a "black matriarchy." As the report revealed neither the strengths nor adaptations developed by the black family since the time of slavery, the ensuing hostility by black leaders and scholars was intense. Joyce Ladner thoughtfully analyzes what some of the repercussions of that intensity may mean for poor black families today:

"The impact of the Moynihan Report was felt long after it was thrust into the national-policy arena. A particularly important reaction to the report was a "closing of the ranks" behind black families among black leaders, policy analysts, and scholars for several years following. There was little public discussion of the problems of black families including the growing problem of teen pregnancy, the increase in female-headed households, and black-on-black crime lest they be guilty of exposing some of the "in-house" problems of blacks to a white society that had already proven to be hostile to the needs and aspirations of black people.

Blacks also reacted strongly to the "social-pathology" label the Moynihan Report applied to the family. This reaction was so strong, it has been suggested, that it led to the creation of a so-called "strengths of black families" body of scholarship in an effort to counteract the impact of those studies which portrayed black families from a negative perspective (Johnson, 1981; Dodson, 1981). This school of thought developed empirically based alternative perspectives and interpretations of black family life that differed sharply from the prevailing social-pathology school of thought.

The strong emphasis on "strengths" of black families as well as an attempt to minimize the escalation of such problems as teen pregnancy, female-headed households, and black-on-black crime, may have unwittingly led to an exacerbation of these problems. During this dormant period the problems worsened. In retrospect, the frontal assault of the Moynihan Report made it impossible for blacks to respond in any other way at the time. It came during the height of the civil-rights movement when blacks were asserting a sense of pride, dignity, and self-worth as they struggled for civil rights. The negative connotation of the report did nothing to promote this sense of urgency for positive social change."

Chapter 6

THE PHYSICALLY DISABLED

In October of 1985, 250 members of the militant group A.D.A.P.T. marched on the Boneventre Hotel. Upon entering the hotel they met security and police resistance. Members of the group blocked elevators and escalators. By the following day the Boneventre had become a police held fortress. Who do you think were the members of this militant and effective group A.D.A.P.T.?[1] Militant blacks demanding jobs, feminist activists calling for increased child care, or physically disabled citizens in wheelchairs who were fed up with inaccessible buildings? It was the latter group that developed this effective action. In fact, during the 1980s many of the most imaginative and effective militant actions have emerged from the physically disabled community. In the early 1980s a number of policy decisions were made that have had a devastating impact upon the physically disabled community. The Reagan Administration and Congress determined in 1981 that between 20% and 30% of all citizens receiving Social Security Disability Insurance (S.S.D.I.) either were ineligible or receiving too large a payment. Those citizens who are defined as being too disabled to participate in the labor force are eligible for S.S.D.I. (a more detailed description of this entitlement will be presented later in the chapter). Consequently, S.S.D.I. has been a life line for a substantial portion of the physically disabled community. The monthly checks distributed through S.S.D.I. have enabled citizens affected by a number of physically disabling diseases or injuries to meet their basic economic needs.

The presumption that between 600,000 and 900,000 recipients were ineligible, however, placed many physically disabled people at risk. The Reagan Administration acted upon this belief and began reviewing S.S.D.I. cases in 1981. Through March of 1984 public officials had reviewed 1,155,000 cases and 485,000 initial notices of termination of benefits were sent out, although half of these terminations were expected to be revised on appeal (Rich, 1984). Former Health and Human Services Secretary Margaret Heckler indicated in February of 1984 that the program would save the 1.1 billion dollars it had projected.

These savings were achieved through an intensified and accelerated process, initiated in March of 1981, which reviewed about 30,000 additional D.I. cases per month, beyond the then-normal workload. The rate of terminations from these reviews was initially close to 50%. In addition, the number of new awards dropped to an all-time low in 1982 with an allowance rate of only 29% of those applying.

As has already been suggested, this review and ultimately budget-cutting process had profound implications for physically disabled citizens. Numbers, however, do not convey the entire story. Newspapers were filled with accounts during this period of disabled veterans, quadriplegics and others who continued to be affected by diseases of the circulatory and musculoskeletal system being summarily and arbitrarily removed from the S.S.D.I. roles. Such decisions were made without face-to-face interviews. Instead, evidence was gathered and determinations made on the basis of case-record material(s). These decisions functioned to heighten the vulnerability of the disabled community and further marginalize the existence of many of its members. Many citizens who either were terminated or rejected from S.S.D.I. during this period had to move in with reluctant families, others were referred back to institutions and some joined the growing ranks of the homeless or committed suicide (Consortium for Citizens with Developmental Disabilities, 1985).

A second threat to the welfare of the physically disabled community also emerged during this period. In the early 1970s, a major piece of legislation, section 504 of the Rehabilitation Act, was enacted. It effectively forbade any type of discrimination against disabled citizens. Strong guidelines were established in the late 1970s, which threatened any federal financial-aid recipient (hospitals, local governments, universities, government assisted developers, etc.) with the withdrawal of such funds if they discriminated against members of the physically disabled community.

These new regulations were intended not only to affect overt discrimination but also to attack more subtle forms of prejudice that denied physically disabled people "access" to a university education, mass transit or housing. In effect, the legislation required institutions receiving federal monies to modify their physical environment for the purpose of making it accessible to physically disabled citizens. Shortly after the ink had dried on this legislation, the Reagan Administration assumed office and determined that these regulations were "too sweepingly stringent and potentially expensive" (Barringer, 1983). The Administration's Task Force on Regulatory Relief was interested in reducing legislative requirements that increased the "cost burden" for federally funded ventures. It identified 504 as a major target for deregulation. The administration specifically intended to narrow the definition of federal financial-aid recipient, restrict the government's authority to make discrimination complaints against such institutions, and give the federal government authority to delegate enforcement to the states (Burress, 1983).

Clearly, these policies would have functioned to reduce the legislative support necessary for disabled citizens to gain or retain entry into the larger society. The disabled community's segregation from mainstream social institutions (schools, jobs, etc.) was in many ways as profound as the discrimination experienced by blacks and latinos. This federal legislation promised to facilitate a process that would enable disabled citizens to integrate with the able-bodied community and relatedly gain their "independence." The directives of the Reagan Administration, however, clearly placed this hope at risk.

The effects of budget retrenchment were also felt by the disabled community in various localities. Cities such as Houston and New York attempted to scale back their efforts to make public transportation accessible. Still other states and municipalities cut back commitments to hiring disabled citizens and developing specialized support services (van services, attendants, and so on). Clearly, the disabled community has been severely threatened by the budget-cutback policies of municipalities, states, and the federal government.

Despite these real and multiple threats, however, disability services and legislation remained virtually intact. Perhaps just as important, certain types of services expanded exponentially during the 1980s. Clearly, there have been areas of retreat and defeat for disabled groups. However, the singular impression during this period is that the "fightbacks" waged by disabled people and their allies have preserved and expanded the base of services. When the federal government threatened to eliminate hundreds of thousands of citizens from the rolls of S.S.D.I., coalitions were formed or reinvigorated and expanded. These groups contacted legislators, media, and other organizations who were sympathetic.

The letter-writing campaigns, lobbying, and heightened visibility were most effective in halting the cuts. For instance, the Consortium for Citizens with Developmental Disabilities and the Coalition to Save our Social Security (comprised of consumer groups, professional associations, and provider agencies) were created to monitor the cutbacks and advance the interests of the disabled. Consumer groups such as Disabled in Action, Eastern Paralyzed Veterans Association, and American Coalition of Citizens with Disabilities functioned independently and also joined these larger efforts to retain the entitlements of disabled citizens.

The clamor raised by these groups had a substantial impact upon the structure of the review process and the rejection and termination rates associated with S.S.D.I. In 1984, more than half the states administering the program for the Social Security Administration (S.S.A.) announced a moratorium on all reviews. Earlier modifications had also been introduced to reduce the so-called insensitivity, inefficiency, and ineffectiveness of these reviews. Congress mandated a face-to-face interview at the first stages of the review process and continued benefits until the appeals judge heard the case. Additionally, a new law was passed stating that "benefits can be terminated by S.S.A. only if there is substantial evidence that the individual's medical condition has improved since first being placed on the rolls and that the individual is capable of working."

Similar coalitions also formed to protect the rights won by disabled citizens under the 504 section of the Rehabilitation Act. This effort was spearheaded by the Disability Rights Education and Defense Fund (D.R.E.D.F.). These advocates called a meeting of nine national organizations that were so preoccupied with fighting budget cuts they could only lend very partial support to this effort. D.R.E.D.F. then turned to local groups of disabled citizens throughout the country. These groups were contacted and subsequently emerged into a grass-roots base of support for D.R.E.D.F.'s efforts to preserve 504.

The Office of Management and Budget noted that "a large constituency had formed which was going to oppose any changes" (Barringer, 1983). This coalition was a diverse group that contained many progressive activists but over time also came to include conservative constituencies such as parents of handicapped children. The pressure applied by this group over an approximate 15-month period caused representatives of the Reagan Administration to withdraw their proposal(s).

It is ironic that perhaps the strongest and most successful battle that has been waged in the 1980s to preserve definitions of entitlement and levels of support services has emerged from the disabled community. Historically, the disabled have been defined individually and collectively by the larger society as inferior and weak. These attitudes have infected every institution within the society. Churches, schools, and businesses consistently either responded to disabled individuals in an overly solicitous manner, which robbed them of their dignity and independence, or simply ignored the disabled person's presence because he or she were not deemed worthy of attention. Pity or scorn were the primary responses of able-bodied citizens when they encountered disabled people. An implicit presumption of these attitudes and behaviors is that disabled people are incapable of functioning in an independent and effective manner.

How odd, then, that the most effective independent battle to stem the tide of budget cuts was waged by the disabled community. Clearly, part of the success of these organizing efforts can be traced to contributions of time, resources, and staff from established agencies such as United Cerebral Palsy and Easter Seals. These professional efforts, however, were only a supplement to the larger grass-roots movement, which was responsible for altering the policies of the Reagan Administration and Congress. This grass-roots movement was largely comprised of disabled people who struggled in the 1970s and 1980s to gain the support services, access, and rights necessary to lead an independent life in the larger able-bodied society. The struggle for independence was marked by the formation of a disabled-rights movement.

The movement in turn created the basis for a new type of service organization, Independent Living Centers. Independent Living Centers are philosophically committed both to providing the support services disabled individuals require (direct services) and modifying environmental barriers that prevent access and thus independence. These service organizations are effectively defined as being an extension of the disabled community and, therefore, require that a majority of the board and substantial proportion of the staff be drawn from this community. It is felt that only in this way can the needs of the community be most effectively identified and met. These organizations' memberships provided much of the critical grass-roots support necessary to preserve and extend services to the physically disabled.

The formation of these alternative or consumer-based organizations represents one of the disabled communities' responses to (1) prevalent prejudices or mythology concerning their condition and (2) the limited definition of need devised by established service agencies. In the next two sections of this chapter we will therefore examine (1) the reality and myths associated with disability and (2) the types of services traditionally available to the physically disabled. Our discussion will establish a context for the emergence of Independent Living Centers. The final section of the chapter will examine the content, structure and scope of Independent Living Centers (I.L.C.). We will more fully review the role ILCs and disabled advocacy organizations played in limiting the impact of budget cuts.

Clearly, other vulnerable groups have much to learn from the disabled community. The successes that they experienced in the 1980s not only to prevent cuts but substantially to increase the funding base of Independent Living Centers is an anomaly. These successes, however, did not occur accidently. Rather, these victories can be traced to the following combination of features, which are characteristic of the new type of agency serving the disabled community (I.L.C.): (1) a membership base; (2) individual need being met through service provision, and (3) vigorous efforts to confront environmental issues that adversely affect membership interests. This vital blend of support, advocacy, and organizing services evolved out of the disabled communities' cumulative, painful encounters with the nondisabled and the institutions that they control.

MYTHOLOGY AND REALITY

As has already been noted the dominant social beliefs and responses to the physically disabled generally function to marginalize their existence. To begin with, there is a strong sense of contagion associated with physical disability. The able-bodied are often frightened to encounter the physically disabled because of the fear that they might contract the disabling disease. This type of reaction is based on misinformation, but it often also forecloses the opportunity to interact with the physically disabled and thus dispel this myth. It has also been suggested that fear of contagion can be traced to the able-bodied person's legitimate concern that physical disability might at some point touch one's life. Rather than confront this fear, nondisabled people too often choose to avoid anything or anyone that reminds them of their vulnerability.

Another myth associated with physical disability is that it represents a punishment for sin. Many fundamentalist groups believe that either in an earlier life or their present life the physically disabled person committed a grievous sin that has essentially been counteracted by God through the disabling disease. This perspective has been growing not diminishing in recent years as fundamentalist groups in this country have experienced a rebirth. This point of view is also being expressed in policymaking circles close to the president. The contention that physical disability can be traced to sin was recently supported by Eileen Gardner, a former U.S. Department of Education official. She noted that:

> The order of the universe is composed of different degrees of development. There is a higher (more advanced) and lower (less advanced). Nothing comes of an individual that he has not (at some point in his development) summoned. . . . As unfair as it may seem a person's external circumstances do fit his level of inner spiritual development. . . Those of the handicapped constituency who seek to have others bear their burdens and eliminate their challenges are seeking to avoid the central issue of their lives [Disability Rights Education and Defense Fund, 1985: 9].

Another strong myth that runs through American culture is that the "disabled are helpless, dependent and inherently inferior" (Asch and Rousso, 1985). We have all been exposed to fundraising drives or literature(s) that depict the physically disabled in the most pitiful and heart-wrenching manner possible. These devices are intended to engage the public's support for the physically disabled. However, these devices also reinforce the belief that the physically disabled are to be pitied because of their disease and relatedly are permanently dependent upon the nondisabled for their continued existence.

This myth also defines encounters between the disabled and non-disabled. If pity is the dominant emotional response and dependence is perceived as the single strongest defining characteristic of the physically disabled, then the nondisabled can be expected to experience much strain and embarrassment in the presence of disabled citizens. This uncomfortable response often contributes to the rejection of the physically disabled person and a desire for economic and social segregation. The prevalent myths of our society have helped shape the nondisabled citizen's attitudes and behavior toward disabled people. This strong belief system has in turn contributed to the formation of two themes that have dominated our social policy toward the physically disabled: segregation and individuated responses to physical circumstance.

The latter point (regarding individuated responses) is most important. If physical disability is exclusively defined as a moral or physiological problem, then social responses will focus on the individual to the exclusion of the environment. In effect, the individual will be held accountable for his or her situation and programs will at best attempt to rehabilitate the individual to make the best adaptation possible to an essentially fixed environment. The presumption that the dilemmas of the physically disabled can be isolated within the individual and are not in part a consequence of the inaccessibility and hostility of the larger environment represents yet another myth.

Finally, it is generally believed that the problem of physical disability touches very few people. In effect physical disability is perceived as a relatively modest problem that is likely to affect only a small fraction of American citizens in their lifetime. Perhaps this belief provides the basis for the nondisabled population's distancing and insulating themselves from the realities associated with physical disability. In any event, it represents one more thread in the mythological tapestry associated with physical disability.

The most recent data suggest that a substantial proportion of Americans are affected by some form of physical disability. The National Health Survey of the Department of H.E.W. reported there was an estimated 29.3 million persons who indicated they were limited in their activities due to chronic illness or impairment. This represents 14.1% of the civilian noninstitutional population of the United States or 14.3 million males and 15 million females (Asch and Rousso, 1985). Additionally, the center estimates that 3.3% of the nation's population or about 6.8 million people are unable to carry on their major activities (Swenyard et al., 1977: 7). This statistic represents 12% of all children, 2.6% of all working-age adults, and 17.1% of all elderly (DeJong, 1983). Clearly, physical disability is affecting a substantial cross section of American citizens.

As these data suggest however, there is a continuum of physical disability. The ends of this spectrum include relatively minor impairments and extreme or severe disabilities. More specifically, minor impairments might include a heart murmur, a limp caused by an earlier bout with polio, or speech impediments; loss of a limb or substantial reduction of mobility due to a stroke are frequently cited as mid-level disabilities; finally, the following are severe disabilities: spinal-cord injury, cerebral palsy, multiple sclerosis, muscular dystrophy and postpolio disablement. The physically disabled are not a homogeneous mass. A range of diseases exist that has affected varying levels of disability.

Many disabled citizens, including those who have experienced relatively minor impairments, and the most severely disabled, have been able to locate employment and live independently. According to a 1978 survey of disability and work, 44% of all citizens with disabilities were employed in the labor market (DeJong, 1983). Some of the explanations cited in the literature for the 56% who are not in the labor market will be identified later in this discussion. Approximately 14% of the severely disabled population was employed. A critical statistic indicates that only 1.5% of the severely disabled are defined as unemployed. Alternatively, approximately 85% of the severely disabled are categorized as being out of the labor force.

The data indicate that substantial numbers of disabled and severely disabled citizens are participating in the labor force. The participation of the disabled in the labor force pierces yet another myth. In fact, many physically disabled citizens are capable of creating and sustaining varying levels of economic independence. Employment has also created the basis for social independence. Many physically disabled citizens may choose not to or be unable to participate in the labor market. Just as important, they may be able to achieve economic independence through S.S.D.I. or other entitlements. In effect, one can achieve economic and social independence without a job. However, it is important to note that many physically disabled people who are willing and able to participate in the labor market have been unable to gain access.

It is this question of access that has continued to plague the disabled community. The problems experienced by disabled citizens as they struggle for employment or other forms of economic and social independence are multiple and can often be traced to an inaccessible environment. How does a disabled person get to work when transportation systems are not modified to enable citizens restricted to a wheelchair or unable to walk ten blocks to a subway or bus to avail themselves of the service? How can disabled people gain access to the skills and technology so necessary to compete in the job market when the university is physically inaccessible? Even if through individual herculean feats a disabled person can contend with inaccessible transportation and university systems, can he or she also overcome the prejudices and discriminatory practices of employers who are unwilling to hire disabled citizens?

Each of these obstacles is located in the environment and effectively represents a triathalon-like contest for the disabled person seeking economic and social independence. Clearly, this reality strikes at the core of two myths associated with physical disability. In fact, the problems of the physically disabled are not primarily a consequence of individual dysfunction or disease. Rather, an at least equally compelling explanation for the continued dependence and isolation of many physically disabled people is that the larger environment is structured to make resources critical to independent living inaccessible. Concomitantly, it is this environmental reality and not qualities intrinsic to physical disability that sustains much of the dependence associated with this group of citizens.

Given the complex social and individual reality associated with physical disability, it is critical that service providers formulate programs that are responsive to the multiple needs of this population. More specifically programs should be organized to address the (1) immediate and physical problems associated with the disease by offering various support services (therapy, income maintenance, individual advocacy, etc.), (2) those parts of the environment that adversely affect disabled citizens, and (3) dispell myths so strongly associated with the physically disabled community. The next section of the chapter will explore the content and structure of services that have traditionally been available to the disabled community.

SERVICES TRADITIONALLY AVAILABLE
TO THE DISABLED COMMUNITY

In general, three types of service agencies have been historically available to the physically disabled. These service-delivery systems might be categorized under the following headings: (1) private philanthropic services, (2) public-direct service programs, and (3) income-maintenance agencies. The particular agencies and types of services associated with these delivery systems will be briefly identified in the following discussion. Just as important, the critical assumptions that unify these otherwise disparate programmatic approaches will also be examined.

Private Agencies. In the United States literally thousands of private agencies that are committed to serving the physically disabled have evolved over the last two centuries. By the twentieth century, most of these organizations maintained specialized interests. For instance, organizations such as the Muscular Dystrophy Association, The Epilepsy Foundation, United Cerebral Palsy, and the American Cancer Society are but a few of the private agencies that have an ongoing interest in a particular disabling disease. The National Rehabilitation Society, the American Occupational Therapy Society, and the National Easter Seals Society for Crippled Children and Adults maintain relatively general disease interests but their preferred methods of intervention remain specialized.

Other agencies such as the Paralyzed Veterans of America and The United Mine Workers Welfare and Retirement Fund are committed to working with groups drawn from particular sectors of the labor force. The specialized focus (disease, intervention, prior occupation) of the private agency is but one of the threads that defines its mission. Additionally, private agencies vary in their scope or size. Most are national organizations with state and local affiliates, some are purely local organizations, and a few maintain international networks. Membership in these organizations total in the hundreds of thousands.

The private agency's sources of fiscal support are multiple. The membership of each of these organizations is expected to contribute directly to agency activities through a monetary pledge. In addition, the membership provides indirect support through various forms of volunteerism. Quite often the private-voluntary agency also receives public support for particular services it offers. For instance, disability research and intensive rehabilitation are often quite expensive. Consequently, the maintenance of the services has recently become quite dependent upon public dollars.

It is becoming increasingly clear that the survival of many voluntary agencies can only be assured through a continuation of public support. Despite this need voluntary agencies in the 1980s have experienced a decline in the amount of real dollars (annual appropriation adjusted for inflation) allocated to their programs. Other revenue sources that have significantly supported the work of these agencies are corporations, foundations, and patrons.

The primary services provided by voluntary agencies are research and rehabilitation. Their research interests might be generally described as medical and technological. Agencies such as United Cerebral Palsy and the Muscular Dystrophy Association support research that is intended to prevent the disease from recurring. Other more technologically focused agencies such as the Rehabilitation Research and Training Centers within various universities "conduct programs . . . aimed toward the discovery of new knowledge which will improve rehabilitation methods . . . alleviate or stabilize handicapping conditions and promote maximum physical, social and economic independence" (Lando et al., 1982).

Additionally, private agencies directly deliver a range of rehabilitation services that include, but are not limited to, (1) vocational rehabilitation, (2) physical therapy, (3) social and psychological services, (4) evaluation of rehabilitation potential, (5) work-adjustment services, and (6) extended employment for those disabled individuals who are not readily absorbed in the competitive labor force (sheltered workshops). In many instances combinations of these services are offered by a single agency.

In general these services are offered by professionals who have been trained in a relatively specialized area of expertise. Each of the service areas associated with the field of physical disability sustains a cadre of specialized professionals. Basic and applied research is conducted by medical doctors. Programs in vocational rehabilitation are often populated by occupational therapists. Alternatively, agencies that focus on the physical rehabilitation of the client generally retain mobility and psychological therapists. To varying extents each of these groups of professionals have been trained in the medical model of service delivery. In effect, the problems of the disabled are defined as being located exclusively within the individual and are therefore treated with specialized knowledge and technology. These techniques are intended to rehabilitate those parts of the individual that are assessed as being most impaired. The treatment interests of professional staff are also greatly defined by the substantive interests, philosophic commitments, and hiring practices of the host agency. Clearly, the medical model's definition of problem and resolution has shaped both agency and professional practice in this arena.

Quite recently a number of disability professional groups and private agencies have begun to redefine their practice. In effect, the exclusive focus upon the individual as repository of the "disability problem" has started to give way to a broader definition, which appreciates the role of the environment in creating and sustaining the dependence of disabled citizens. This shift can in great part be traced to pressure(s) exerted by consumer groups and will be discussed at greater length in the final section of this chapter.

Public Agencies. There are a variety of publicly funded direct services that have been targeted at the disabled community. As has already been suggested a number of services such as vocational rehabilitation and research are subcontracted through private agencies. Other services are delivered directly by public agencies, such as the Veterans Administration, to the target population. Two of the oldest service commitments of the government are to disabled veterans and vocational rehabilitation. In the nineteenth century these twin commitments greatly overlapped. Much of the government's expenditures on vocational rehabilitation was to veterans who had been scarred by war. More recently, however, the public sector has made a differentiated investment in disabled civilian and veteran populations.

During the course of the twentieth century there has been much legislation that has focused on the delivery and organization of vocational rehabilitation services. Over time this legislation (1) expanded eligibility for these services, (2) recreated federal, state, and local relationships (more support for states with larger populations), (3) funded innovative and experimental programs, (4) subsidized physical-construction projects, and (5) increased the financial base of these services. What has essentially remained constant, however, is the critical philosophical underpinning of this legislation and its core services.

Vocational-rehabilitation services consistently have been intended to reintegrate disabled citizens into the labor force. For instance, in 1948 it was noted "that the most economic approach of meeting the situation [needs of the disabled] is an appropriate program of vocational rehabilitation. When a disabled person may be made fit to employ through rehabilitation and become a tax producer rather than a tax consumer, it would seem poor economy to deny him the necessary services. This is the dollars and cents justification of the program" (Fay, 1977: 299).

This general principle has changed very little in four decades. In effect it has defined as "success" the number of people who were gainfully employed subsequent to experiencing the program. Relatedly, it targeted those likely to "benefit" from the program. Vocational-rehabilitation programs focused on disabled individuals gaining the necessary skills or information to enter the labor market. Again, the individual is defined as the locus of the problem. Finally, the vocational-rehabilitation agency is "required to rehabilitate a maximum number of disabled to retain its appropriation and support which in turn has resulted in quotas being imposed upon vocational counselors" (Obermann, 1965: 296).

A major concern about the structure of vocational-rehabilitation services is that it has led to a numbers game. Too often vocational counselors seem preoccupied with "easy rehabs" so that they can meet their quotas. Consequently, the program has been accused of creaming (selecting in only those most likely to succeed) and concomitantly denying services to the most severely disabled. This point is underscored by a study of the Urban Institute, which estimated that only 2% of the total public allocation to the severely disabled was spent on vocational-rehabilitation services (Fay, 1977: 294).

The effectiveness of vocational rehabilitation has been affected by the declining real-dollar outlay for these services in the 1980s. Budget allocations have always been a problem as evidenced by vocational-rehabilitation programs only reaching 120,000 of the 10 million severely disabled in 1975. This ratio has been reduced in the 1980s because of the program's standstill budget, which represents a loss of real dollars. In sum, although vocational-rehabilitation services are a vital element in the constellation of services available to the disabled community, their effectiveness has been impaired by an exclusive emphasis upon individual dysfunction, preoccupation with quotas, and relatively modest budget.

Another substantial public program providing direct services to the disabled community is the Veterans Administration. The Veterans Administration reaches millions of disabled vets. It provides care in hospitals, outpatient clinics, nursing homes, and institutions. Some of its services include (1) vocational and occupational therapy, (2) funds for adaptive equipment and housing, and (3) comprehensive health care. The veteran must meet certain criteria before he or she is eligible for services. In general all veterans are eligible for these services but certain groups do receive a higher priority than others. For instance, veterans who require hospitalization because of any injuries or diseases incurred in the line of duty receive top priority from intake personnel.

A problem that has received attention from the V.A. is spinal-cord injuries. During the past decade a relatively substantial investment has been made to expand existing services and create new facilities for this population. During the 1970s and 1980s a rather comprehensive network of spinal-cord injury centers has emerged. These centers emphasize physical, vocational, and community-oriented rehabilitation. Much of this expansion can be traced to groups such as the Eastern Paralyzed Veterans Association, documenting the problems associated with present patterns of care and advocating for particular policy and programmatic changes.

It is interesting to note the Veterans Administration's budget has been quite insulated from the climate of retrenchment during the 1980s. Compared with other programs, the V.A. fared quite well between 1981 and 1985. Similar to other agencies serving the disabled, the V.A.'s organization and delivery of services is predicated upon principles of the medical model.

Income-Maintenance Programs. A variety of entitlement programs are available to disabled citizens. Clearly, food stamps, Medicare, and Medicaid are essential entitlements available to subgroups within the disabled community. Social Security Supplemental Security Income is a program of direct benefits available to "totally disabled individuals who on the basis of their monthly income are below a certain level of support" (Fay, 1977: 294). The projected annual budget allocation for S.S.I. was approximately 9 billion dollars in 1985. By far, the most critical direct payment or income-maintenance entitlement available to the disabled community is Social Security Disability Insurance (S.S.D.I.) which provides cash payments "to eligible persons and their dependents when the covered person suffers . . . impairment that has lasted or is expected to last 12 months or more and the impairment prevents any substantial employment" (p. 292). The projected allocation for this program was $19 billion in F.Y.A. 1985.

As has already been noted, in the 1980s S.S.D.I. has been subjected to close security and substantial cutbacks. In effect, there was an accelerated review of S.S.D.I. recipients and applicants. Eligibility and continued benefits have remained dependent upon medical or clinical definitions of disability. As Deborah Stone (1984: 87) noted in *The Disabled State,* "it is remarkable how that faith in clinical judgment persisted. . . . One can only marvel—or despair—at the technicalization of a political issue."

Until very recently medical definitions of eligibility provided the basis for the expansion of this program. During the 1980s, however, there has been an intensified effort by federal policy makers to restrict medical definitions of eligibility and thus costs. The fate of S.S.D.I. is critical to the disabled community inasmuch as millions of recipients' economic survival is intertwined with the fate of this entitlement.

Perhaps more important than any single entitlement or program was the response of large segments of the disabled community in the 1970s and 1980s to the panoply of services available to disabled citizens. As we noted earlier, consumers were critical of these programs' exclusive emphasis upon individual dysfunction and their related failure to identify and respond to environmental impediments that denied disabled citizens access to critical services, skills, or employment. These environmental obstacles were defined by consumers as the critical explanatory variable for the continued economic and social dependence of many disabled citizens.

Consumer groups indicated that the professional bases of practice in the area of disability too often missed the primary issues affecting the lives of disabled citizens. They also suggested that too often traditional service agencies either segregated the disabled in sheltered workshops and housing or, at the other extreme, placed the individual in the position of having to make all the necessary adaptations to the environment if he or she wanted to live independently. The latter pattern, it was argued frequently, resulted in the provision of services to the least disabled citizens.

Ironically, the most severely disabled people were effectively denied such services because they were defined as least likely to make the adjustments necessary to function independently (housing, employment, and so on). These entrenched patterns of service delivery in combination with public allocations that fell far short of meeting the most basic needs of the disabled community functioned as a catalyst for action in the 1970s and 1980s. The disabled communities' response(s) to the traditional service system's failure to meet basic need was to create alternate service organizations. Just as important, disabled citizens concurrently created advocacy organizations. However, it is the Independent Living Center (or alternate service formulation) which is of primary interest to this discussion. The context, structure effectiveness, tensions, and hopes of these new service organizations will provide a basis for the remainder of the discussion in this chapter.

THE INDEPENDENT LIVING MOVEMENT

In the late 1960s and early 1970s a variety of forces sparked the Independent Living Movement. The civil-rights struggle of blacks and Hispanics contributed toward shaping the tactics and focus of the movements' early organizations. The movement was particularly concerned with entitlement benefits and civil rights. Antidiscrimination legislation functioned as a focal point for much of the organizing in the disabled community during this period. Particular emphasis was placed on the most critical and entrenched areas of discrimination in the job and housing markets. Benefit rights were defined as prerequisites to living in a community setting. Consequently, the availability of adequate benefits and support services was an equally compelling agenda item in the early stages of this movement. Organizations such as Disabled in Action (D.I.A.), The Eastern Paralyzed Veterans, and the American Coalition of Citizens with Disabilities (A.C.C.D.) staged rallies, sit-ins, and other demonstrations in order to underscore forcefully specific discriminatory practices and benefit needs.

This movement, however, was equally invested in developing new service models and delivery systems for the disabled community. As has already been noted, many of the features of these services evolved as a response to the practices of traditional service agencies. The independent living centers (I.L.C.) consistently focused on issues of critical importance to the disabled community that were characteristically either ignored or relegated to a status of secondary importance by private and public-service agencies.

In general, centers attempted to (1) offer the concrete support services and (2) facilitate the development of environmental modifications necessary for disabled people to live independently in their own communities. The earliest I.L.C. in Berkeley, California, which functioned as a model for the entire movement, required that the organization be controlled by consumers. This requirement and a later legislative mandate indicated that at least 50% of the board and a substantial proportion of the center's staff be drawn from the disabled community.

Consumer control was a critical feature of the I.L.C. as envisioned by its earliest practitioners. Such control was intended to assure that the center's primary services were developed on the basis of the perceived needs of the disabled community. Just as important, this alternate structure was expected to facilitate the

development of leadership and practice skills, thus further reen-
forcing the drive toward community independence. The structure
and services of centers were also shaped by the concurrent drives
in the larger society for self-care (demedicalization), self-help,
and consumer control(s).

The early philosophic commitment(s) of the I.L.C. movement
was to focus on a neglected area of the disabled person's experience, his or her interaction with the larger environment. Therefore
services were organized to enable the disabled to gain access to the
larger society. The larger environment was identified as the handicapping factor. Architectural designs for buildings, transportation
systems, and employment practices created barriers and thus
denied the disabled community access to the larger environment.
These obstacles tended to segregate disabled citizens. It was on this
basis that access and integration became two of the seminal con-
cepts of the movement. The objective of this segment of the disabled community was to normalize the environment and make it
accessible.

The movement also struggled to redefine the role of the disabled
citizen from client to consumer and ultimately provider. To cope
with environmental barriers it has been indicated that the disabled
person must shed the relatively passive client/patient role for the
more assertive consumer role. DeJong (1983) has noted that it is
only the consumer role which will enable disabled citizens to begin
addressing the structural obstacles which are daily influencing
their lives. The full development of disabled individuals and their
communities requires that they acquire the skills necessary to meet
their own needs. This skill development is expected to be facilitated through mutual-aid and self-help projects. Consistent with
the philosophical underpinnings of the movement such services are
intended to reduce dependence on medical professionals and build
on the strengths of disabled people.

In the early 1970s the Independent Living Movement spawned
a number of centers. The most notable were located in Berkeley,
Boston, and Brooklyn. These centers did not offer a uniform package of services. Rather, some such as the Boston center emphasized residential housing services while others such as Berkeley
organized their services around nonresidential services. However,
the 504 section of the Vocational Rehabilitation Act (1973, 1978)
which provides federal funding for the creation of centers established many of its criteria from the Berkeley model. This legislation and state laws most notably in California, New York, and

Massachussetts enforce features that require consumer control, mutual-aid projects, and advocacy.

Within this legislative framework, however, there continues to be much room for difference(s) between Independent Living Centers. Some centers choose to emphasize peer counseling and training in independent-living skills. Peer counseling is an example of consumer involvement or mutual aid. In effect, disabled peers, on staff or voluntarily, provide critical counseling services to consumers. Independent-living skills are used to develop self-direction rather than task-oriented behavior capability as has traditionally occurred. Self-direction skills that are emphasized include judgement, persistence, memory, consistency of behavior, accurate perception of capabilities, and limits.

These skills in turn become the basis for contributing to the emotional and physical development of the disabled person in the areas of mobility, functional skills, sexuality, and education. Other centers have chosen to emphasize advocacy, community consultation, or education. Still others focus on attendant care, financial-aid counseling, mobility training, and transportation services. Attendant care is one of the services most closely associated with the I.L.C., especially with regard to severely disabled persons. Attendant care is intended to provide ongoing routine care as an alternative to institutionalization.

The Independent Living Center model of attendant care functions as an alternative to the medical model's definition of the service. Again, the disabled person is a consumer (not a patient) and this controls the hiring and firing of personnel as well as the content of the service. The service is not necessarily seen as episodic and, therefore, dependent on a crisis, but continuous, thus supporting the disabled person's daily struggle for independence. Finally, one of the most frequently cited services provided by centers is housing (owned and operated by the I.L.C.).

This service offers accessible housing to the disabled community. On average, the budget for an I.L.C. is between 100,000 and 150,000 dollars. The nonresidential center serves approximately 500 members, while the residential center addresses the needs of approximately 50 members. Combinations of this variety of services are offered without violating the basic principles of the Independent Living Movement (I.L.M.).[2]

The most critical constituent group in the early stages of the movement for such services was the severely disabled citizen. More specifically, young adults with spinal-cord injuries, muscular dystrophy, cerebral palsy, multiple sclerosis, and postpolio disablement were the core groups of this movement. This group's early mass support and ongoing leadership has been traced to their (1) historic lack of access to a range of rehabilitation services, (2) greater ability to organize around issues because they were relatively free from economic and familial responsibilities, and (3) greater numbers in university communities where the movement first took root.

Such groups, organizing in the early and late 1970s, contributed to the creation and enforcement of legislation (Vocational Rehabilitation Act sections 501-504) that assured access to universities, transportation systems, and housing. This legislation provided the seed money for Independent Living Centers (I.L.C.). Local organizing particularly in California, Michigan, and New York resulted in the development of similar legislation at a state level. It is important to reiterate that this effort was spearheaded by both advocacy organizations (D.I.A., E.P.V.A, and A.C.C.D.) and Independent Living Centers. These organizations' membership provided much of the grass-roots support for this legislation. For instance, in the late 1970s rallies and demonstrations were organized in San Francisco, Chicago. New York, and Washington, D.C. to dramatize the Carter Administration's nonenforcement of this legislation.

By 1979, the Carter Administration was vigorously enforcing this legislation and the number of I.L.C.s had quadrupled from approximately 8 to 32. During the 1980s the I.L.M. has scored a number of surprising and unique victories. To begin with, the total number of I.L.C.s continues to mushroom. In 1985, the Independent Living Research Utilization Project has estimated that 150 Independent Living Centers, the practices of which are generally consistent with principles of the movement (consumer control, an emphasis on access, the development of services that encourage mutual aid and integration) had been established throughout the country. A few specific illustrations underscore the magnitude of this expansion.

Between 1979 and 1985 the number of Independent Living Centers increased from 1-12 in Colorado; 16-31 in California; 3-13 in Florida; and 7-26 in New York. Much of this expansion can be traced to specific states independently allocating increased resources toward the creation of I.L.C.s. Additionally, the federal investment increased between 1979 and 1985 from approximately $1.5 million to $27 million. Much of the impetus for this expansion was due to the advocacy efforts and arguments of economic efficiency developed by grass-roots groups and service-agency coalitions. Independent Living Centers were increasingly being presented to legislators as a relatively inexpensive alternative to institutionalization. During this period a National Coalition of Independent Living Centers (N.C.I.L.C.), staffed almost entirely on a voluntary basis, emerged to lobby for the interests of centers.

The philosophy and practice of Independent Living Centers provided the basis for much of the grass-roots support necessary to defend civil-rights legislation, entitlements, and services from attack in the 1980s. The emphasis upon (1) consumer control, (2) advocacy, attendant, peer, and other services that are organized to facilitate self-determination (consumers defining and acting on issues that are critical in their lives), and (3) environmental barriers, which diminish the potential of the disabled community, was critical to the development of this grass-roots movement.

Independent Living Centers are perhaps the primary organizational mechanism for expressing these ideas. The service content and structure of many centers has enabled some consumers to understand the relationship between the climate of retrenchment and their fate. More concretely, it is expected that if a center emphasizes through its daily activities the equally important role of direct services (such as attendant care and peer counseling) and environmental change (lobby, testimony, etc.) in shaping the lives of its members, individuals and groups will be influenced by this service experience. It is anticipated that this service model by highlighting (through the structure of its practice) the critical relationship between the environment and personal struggles for self-determination, will activate members to recognize and defend their interests.

To some extent this worked in the 1980s. Clearly, the nature of this involvement has been altered during the past decade. Disabled citizens are no longer as likely to engage in militant actions to protect their benefits, rights, and services. Rather, they engage in more negotiatory forms of advocacy. Grass-roots involvement has specifically taken the form of letter writing, phone calling, and legislative lobbying. In effect, negotiation replaced militance. Additionally, Independent Living Centers and progressive-advocacy organizations such as D.R.E.D.F., D.I.A., and A.C.C.D. formed new coalitions with traditionally conservative groups such as mothers of handicapped children.

These new coalitions in combination with the tactics of negotiation have been relatively effective in halting the effort to retrench

benefits and rights available to the disabled community and creating the basis for the expansion of other services, most notably
Independent Living Centers. It is also important to note that these
coalitions progressed beyond the characteristically defensive posture of service groups during this period by supporting efforts
that were intended to advance the rights of disabled citizens. For
instance, in 1982 a judicial decision in New York State guaranteed
disabled citizens certain access rights to transportation. More militant tactics (including rallies, demonstrations, and sit-ins) are currently being employed for access rights to transportation by the
A.D.A.P.T. coalition in the mid- and far west. I.L.C.s in the western part of the country have made significant contributions to this
coalition.

Despite the many contributions of Independent Living Centers
they are currently experiencing a range of critical tensions. To
begin with, their relatively modest total budget(s) cannot begin to
address even a fraction of the total need in the disabled community.
This problem is similar to the tension experienced by vocational-
rehabilitation programs, although it should be noted that the centers have not creamed but rather directed their services at the most
severely disabled groups. The increased dependence of many centers upon public monies may ultimately threaten their advocacy
role.

The question, of course, is how long will the government fund
organizations that directly and indirectly press for increased public
expenditures for social services. Another tension is that a number
of centers (not included in the 150 count) have recently emerged
that define themselves as I.L.C.s but violate critical principles of
the movement. The tendencies of these centers has been to vest
relatively substantial authority in professionals and pay little attention to access issues. Relatedly, a number of centers that were initially committed to the general principles of the Berkeley model
are experiencing certain pressure(s) to professionalize.

These pressures can in part be traced to the preferences of certain funding sources, professionally trained disabled workers, and
board members in conflict about their role(s) and the expectations
of clients/consumers who have been socialized to a professional
system. Additionally, the vitality and growth of I.L.C.s has on
occasion been at the expense of independent disabled-advocacy
groups. Many of the I.L.C.'s activist volunteers, board members,
and workers have been drawn from these advocacy organizations.
The relatively small pool of activists, their limited time, and increas-

ing investment in I.L.C.s has impaired the effectiveness of organizations like D.I.A. and A.C.C.D.

This is a critical issue because advocacy organizations often helped to spearhead efforts to resist retrenchment. If this diminution of support continues, the entire disabled community may be increasingly vulnerable to budget cutbacks. Another tension is the tendency of many I.L.C.s to focus increasingly on the delivery of concrete self-help/mutual-aid services to the disabled, while paying less attention to access/environmental issues. Over time, centers are increasingly defining themselves as direct-service providers. Again, if this trend continues, it would duplicate the traditional service providers' tendency to ignore environmental issues and exclusively focus on service provision to the individual.

The models of service delivery might differ, but the fundamental process and outcome of defining the individual as the repository of the problem would remain constant. Just as clearly, this drift would also heighten the vulnerability of the disabled community to future cuts, because the intimate connection(s) between the need for environmental modification and membership activity would be lost. In effect, the absence of grass-roots constituent support to protect the interests of the disabled community (so prevalent among other threatened service providers) would accompany this shift in structure.

Many other tensions too numerous to identify are currently being experienced by I.L.C.s. In great part, these tensions can be traced to the fact that this service formulation represents a departure from many of the primary trends in service delivery, i.e., professionalization, exclusive focus upon the individual as the source of the problem, hierarchical relationships, and distance from the targeted community. The emphasis upon consumer control, mutual aid, and the environment (as the primary repository of the problem) represents a major break with these patterns.[3]

It is this formulation that accounts for many of the individual and collective successes of the disabled community in meeting its membership's needs. At their best, I.L.C.s only meet a small fraction of individual need. However, these centers provided much of the basis for preserving and expanding available services to the disabled. This was accomplished through the creation of services that facilitated the involvement of consumers in their own lives and the lives of their community. The future capacity of the disabled community to resist budget cuts and advance certain rights or meet basic need, may be critically intertwined with the fate of these centers. How the already cited pressures to conform to traditional patterns of service delivery are managed may ultimately determine the future strength(s) of the disabled community. This experience within the disabled community offers a number of critical lessons for maintaining and advancing the rights of a range of vulnerable groups in the 1980s. The future strength of other vulnerable groups may well depend on their capacity to adopt this general model to meet specific need.

NOTES

1. A.D.A.P.T. stands for Association for the Disabled for Accessible Public Transportation.
2. The section 8 requirements for housing assistance do limit I.L.C. occupants to income ceilings in the mid $20,000 range. Scott Smith, disabled Hunter College student and activist, reminded us that such regulations "allow independence - but only so much." Our thanks to him for identifying this limitation.
3. We address these issues and tensions again in the final chapter when we explore new models of advocacy and service.

APPENDIX 1:
Exercises:
To reflect on your attitudes toward
particular groups of disabled citizens

(1a) In general, do you feel uncomfortable encountering and interacting with particular groups of disabled people? If so, specify the groups (quadriplegics, amputees, cancer victims, etc.). Describe your feelings and behavior.
(1b) Do you generally consider the disabled or subgroups of disabled citizens as permanently dependent? If so, specify the subgroup, the presumed area(s) of permanent dependence (work, play, sexuality, etc.), and moments in your life when "individuals departed from this anticipated pattern of dependence and functioned independently." Did these independent behaviors cause you to reflect on your beliefs (concerning the dependence of this disabled group)? If so, explain.
(1c) Have you observed individuals/institutions etc. engaging in practices that diminished and discriminated against disabled

citizens? Specify the incident and describe your response or feelings.

(1d) What are the forces in your social world that perpetuate the attitudes and behaviors identified in questions 1a, b, and c. Specify how and why these prejudices are perpetuated in your family, church, school, etc.

(1e) How in your daily life can you begin to work to break this cycle of prejudice? Specify. Are you prepared to engage in this type of activism? What type of supports would you require to engage in such risk taking?

(1f) What types of devices have you relied upon to distance yourself from the problems of the disabled?

(2a) Have there been moments or periods in your life when you felt relatively disabled (sports, social relationships, school, family)? How did you feel in relationship to others who defined you as disabled (angry, inferior, distanced)? Why?

(2b) What behaviors would you have appreciated from family, friends, acquaintances, and so on? When such behaviors were expressed did they affect your attitudes and actions? Alternatively, what behaviors upset you the most? How did they influence your sense of self and behavior?

(2c) Did you form friendships with others who had a similar disability? How did the members of this group support each other? Did you identify and address environmental factors that affected your functioning? If so, explain.

APPENDIX 2:
Direct Practice Questions

(1) Describe the difference in role(s) between a patient and consumer.

(2) Describe the strengths and weaknesses of a rehabilitation or medical model of practice.

(3) Identify and describe the struggles, frustrations, and so on, associated with your daily practice. Have these issues recently intensified?

(4) Why is it particularly critical that environmental issues be incorporated into practice models and acted upon during this period of retrenchment?

(5) Identify concrete ways in which you can begin to make organic connections in your daily practice between individual and environmental factors. How can you begin to act even modestly on this connection?
(6) Identify practice approaches that reinforce the dependence of clients. Specify approaches that are intended to facilitate a process of self-determination or independence (as described in this chapter).
(7) Are you incorporating mutual aid and self-help approaches in your daily practice? Why? Why Not? How can you initiate such a process?

Too often social service practitioners fail to look at the role of the environment in shaping practice choices. Just as important, the role of the client in the process of change is often ignored. It is particularly critical during this period of diminishing resources that the practitioner struggles to identify the manner in which the environment is defining particular problems and the role the client can play to affect individual and collective change. Clearly, overworked social-service staff cannot independently affect such change. A critical question then for the social service worker is how to create processes that enable clients to take control of their own lives and communities.

Chapter 7

THE NEW UNEMPLOYED

Cultural and economic life often are more intertwined than we imagine. In the late 1800s, the mythic figures of young men moving from "rags to riches" developed by Horatio Alger helped propagate the belief that inevitable material success came from innate ability, hard work, and only just a touch of luck for any boy in America. Serving as a cultural icon for the swift and often rapacious rise of industrialists and robber barons, the Horatio Alger stories gave dreams to millions, and an excuse for those successful few to ignore all those left behind. Whatever the degree of fiction, its cultural power took a grip on American consciousness that didn't lessen for generations.

Designed primarily for white Anglo-Saxon Protestants, this myth of vast individual success was measured in the never-never land of millionaires. Its imagery complemented the philosophical and economic arguments of Social Darwinism and the "laws of the economic jungle" (Trattner, 1974: chap. 5) popular in the nineteenth century. By the mid-twentieth century, the huge tides of European immigrants and the emancipation of slaves, combined with new economic demands for a larger, more skilled, labor force created impulses toward new mythic figures (Braverman, 1974: esp. chaps. 1 and 2). Such figures had to accommodate the members of a vastly more hetergeneous and more educated populous, who knew they could never attain vast wealth but expected security and comfort. By the 1950s, the figure who came to embody a new version of the American dream was no millionaire; it was the industrial worker of the northeast and midwest. This figure held out a seemingly more realistic promise to millions who hoped for a nice house, a nice car or two, and security in old age. Horatio Alger had been replaced by the auto worker.

If one looked at an auto worker—or for that matter, almost any unionized manufacturing worker—the myth seemed to be true. In 1968, the average white male auto worker made over $10,000 a year (with overtime, of course); by 1985's standards that is about $28,000 a year, plus benefits (Bluestone and Harrison, 1982: chaps. 1-3). According to UAW reports, their pension funds were among the richest in the nation; medical benefits were improving, and unemployment compensation so good that if workers were laid off they received both unemployment checks and subs, supplemental unemployment benefits totaling 95% of their previous weekly wage. As layoffs were never long enough for a serious crunch, the nicely framed home, gleaming two-car garages, and motorboats were enjoyed without serious economic strain. (This rosy picture, it needs to be stressed, even when accurate, does not include how hard the labor was, how alienating and contentious the conditions under which workers labored, or how often strikes and work stoppages were necessary to win these material gains.) While there was no significant wealth or summer estates to pass on, the union member could pass on his union card with the promise of a decent living from one generation to the next. America, the land of upward mobility and the solidly middle class, had a myth of great power that excited the imagination of poor people worldwide: the middle-class worker.

It was, of course, a white male myth, no longer WASP but Slavic, Irish, and Italian. (It should be remembered as well that the majority of *all* white male workers—nonunionized, nonmanufacturing—made much less income.) Some blacks and a few Hispanics managed to get a portion of the dream, but only about 57% of it according to Bureau of Labor Statistics through the early 1970s. That meant lower-paying, less-skilled jobs, less security, and, given continuing discrimination and redlining, inferior housing (Bluestone and Harrison, 1982). Women weren't even part of the myth, except as caretakers inside that picket fence. Only after the social movements of the 1960s and early 1970s were these groups allowed initial access to these higher wages and benefits.

As we recounted in chapter one, the economic props to this myth fell apart in the 1970s. The effect on the industrial workers in manufacturing was tremendous and, relative to their previous economic and social conditions, perhaps more precipitous than for any group we are examining here. As numerous statistics attest, the job loss in major manufacturing industries like auto, steel, and rubber have been enormous: Over 1,834,000 manufacturing jobs have been lost and not replaced since 1979 alone (White, 1984). Membership in major industrial unions is down as well: 300,000 in auto, 670,000 lost in steel. Overall, unemployment in former manufacturing states such as Michigan is still at 10%. By 1982, the popular image of the middle-class worker had been replaced with the more disconcerting sight of a new archetype: *the new unemployed*.

The new unemployed were workers who were once perceived as well off and who had never experienced consistent unemployment. They now faced the likelihood of a drastically reduced standard of living for the rest of their lives. Their numbers seem increasingly larger, for the unemployment percentage referred to in the previous paragraph can be misleading. That figure of 10% unemployed in Michigan is based on *only those actively seeking employment*. "Discouraged workers," estimated at over 1,295,000 people in official government statistics and as high as 4 million workers by other experts (Bluestone and Harrison, 1982), are workers who have looked for jobs without success for so long that they stop looking due to such ongoing failure. The once-comfortable manufacturing worker used to 40 hours of decent-paying wages often finds himself or herself in this category. Strapped with large monthly payments on no-longer new cars and homes, they see no worth in fast-food chains or other dead-end minimum-wage jobs. These new poor are often not in a social or psychological position to start over at such menial levels of employment that hold no promise for advancement (Noble, 1985).

As for the now popular argument that people can be trained for comparable jobs in the ever-expanding services sector, a more careful look at wage and hourly rates reveals a sharp difference in income potential for today's service worker. As the Bureau of Labor Statistics (1985) reveals, the hourly wages in retail trade are 62.9% of the hourly wage in manufacturing; the hourly wages in finance, insurance, real estate and other services are 83.2%. Because so much more of this work is part time, *weekly* wages are even lower: in finance, real estate, and insurance, 75.3%; in retail trade, 46.5%; and in "other services," 67.7% of the weekly wages in manufacturing. Income is falling behind faster in these areas, with underemployment and the exhausting need for "doubling up" (holding two part-time jobs) far greater than in the past.

The pain of either long-term unemployment or exhausting under-employment was not felt initially by many unionized manufacturing workers. Their transition from the ranks of the fully employed to the lines of the unemployed was smoothed over through supplemental benefits provided by the federal government when their state's benefits ran out. In general, the group taking most advantage of the 8- to 14-week extension was older, whiter, and more male than those who received only state unemployment checks for the maximum 40-week period (Noble, 1985). This suggests the inability of the new unemployed to locate work of any kind, meaning that their numbers would soon be part of the discouraged-worker pool. (Unemployment statistics need to be understood on many levels, such as regional. Equally important, the historical trend is toward higher and higher figures of unemployment at the end of each major recession: after 1948-1949, only 2.8% unemployed; 1953-1954, 3.6%; 1960-1961, 4.5%; 1969-1970, 5.2%; 1973-1975, 6.2%; 1980, 7.1%. The percentage of Americans unemployed is getting larger all the time.)

At this writing, the national figure for unemployment is 7.2% (double that for blacks and Hispanics). It is a remarkable figure both for its size and for the lack of protest that such a figure would have created at any other time in our history. A New York Times analysis of unemployment and protest suggests that this lack of militant protest from even the official trade-union leadership means a historic retreat by government from its long-standing commitment to keeping unemployment at 4% (New York Times, 1985).

Some of the reasons relate to demographic shifts. The successful fights by blacks, Hispanics, and women to enter the officially documented (and better-paid) labor force, the flood of post-World War II "baby boomers" onto the job market, and the desire of many seniors to continue working past age 65, have all affected employment figures. But what is of equal and more ominous magnitude is the government's tremendous emphasis on budget reduction over any form of nondefense spending, which has ruled out significant job-training efforts for the unemployed. Supplemental benefits were terminated in 1985, and job training, especially for the new unemployed, do not exist on a national scale (Noble, 1985). The result is a continuing level of suffering for this segment of the unemployed who, no longer seeing themselves as representatives of the American dream, are fighting to simply "hold on to what we had," as one Pittsburgh steel worker put it at an unemployed council meeting in 1985.

MENTAL-HEALTH INTERVENTIONS
WITH THE NEW UNEMPLOYED

However, before we return to look at the types of activity many of the new unemployed have developed to maintain their standard of living, we need to look at how these once-successful industrial workers have responded to services designed to help them lessen the stress of long-term unemployment. It would seem natural that their need for social services, counseling, and other mental-health and health-related services would be high. After all, the prospect of downward mobility and permanent underemployment should create understandable strains in personal, family, and community living where few had been before.

One working with the new unemployed will find sharp differences from other groups in need of services. Such differences dramatically effect the type of services and advocacy one can expect to engage in successfully. It must be remembered that the newly unemployed steel worker or auto worker most likely does not have the chronic work problems in her or his past (especially if the worker is a white male). There will be little cultural or ideological support for accepting services. Second, these individuals may have had no direct dealings with the welfare state, other than perhaps either brief hospitalizations, which were covered by union benefits or trips to the unemployment line during relatively short layoffs. The sense of self-reliance engendered by years of maintaining a living wage and by cultural artifact may make them initially very suspicious of the other, welfare-state based services and entitlements such as food stamps, mental-health care, and the like. Any service worker needs to approach newly unemployed workers with an awareness of their less-than-benign attitudes toward social services (Buss et al., 1983).

Such conclusions are at the centerpiece of a thorough two-year study on mental-health services offered to laid-off workers in Youngstown, Ohio, one of the former centers of the steel industry. The work makes clear that laid-off steel workers in both the short term (less than three months) and long run (two years) were *actively* disinterested in receiving mental-health services of any kind that were proffered by area agencies to help lessen the shock of long-term, widespread unemployment.

The study is a sobering account of the detailed outreach efforts begun by community-based satellite clinics that ended two years later in vast underutilization of services by steel workers and their families and frustration on the part of the service workers. Regardless of the approach, from decentralized store-front programs to standard bureaucratic entitlement procedures, the lack of response led the authors to conclude that service intervention *per se* was not an effective approach for engaging new unemployed workers in community or mental-health issues (Buss et al., 1983: 174-186). As the authors suggested, even with serious, innovative interventions in neighborhood clinics, these services remained unattractive because they threatened the still high self-esteem of the laid-off steel workers. That the coping mechanism of greatest preference for stress reduction was the increased use of alcohol (p. 176) gives one an idea of how actively disengaged from mental-health services these workers were. As the Youngstown researchers found, there were so many years of previous indifference to such services that the overwhelming number of respondents never thought of social services as a mechanism available to them for help during a time of need. Of the less than 10% who did seek help, the majority of them did not return after one visit, feeling the bureaucratic paperwork too demeaning and embarrassing to tolerate (p. 144). The overwhelming majority preferred approaching their problems in different ways. In short, "service work," as one thinks of the term when related to other economically distressed groups, does not yet meaningfully exist for the new unemployed.

It is thus no accident that the vast amount of work in which the new unemployed are engaged is far more collectively focused, more political, and more conflictive than almost any work with the new American poor. For unlike hunger, the cause of their problems is more readily apparent: the closing down or drastic restructuring of their workplace. This stark economic reality often places them in direct confrontation with other social groups in their community or region: owners, plant managers, and major politicians. Unlike others who have learned to accept (if not totally enjoy) the benefits of the welfare state and its services, the new unemployed have directed their efforts in two complementary directions: in the long run, the finding of new, equally productive jobs and, in the short run, the retention of their homes and social networks within their communities. While no longer in mythic proportions, they want their particular dreams to keep living for themselves and their children.

Such objectives may help explain why welfare-state services are so unpopular: the new unemployed's perception that the welfare state can not find any well-paying jobs or keep their mortgaged homes is correct. For the newly unemployed manufacturing worker, the approach has been one of either a high-risk, individualized attempt to "strike it rich" (or at least "strike it middle class") in new areas of the country, or, failing that, to stay put and join in with the efforts of other workers and community members to revitalize the community in which they live.

The individual approach seemed most popular between 1976 and 1981 (Bluestone and Harrison, 1982). During these years, the combination of steel-town blues and oil-field booms created a powerful image of sun-belt prosperity that many former manufacturing workers found hard to resist. Unfortunately, the overexpansion of oil facilities worldwide and the continuing decline in America's industrial advantage with other Third World nations, all culminating in the disastrous 1981-1982 recession, led to drastic cuts in sunbelt industries as well. The workers first let go were often those last hired—the transplanted workers of the midwest and northeast. Now living far from their communities of origin and lacking the concomitant supports such roots create, many of these workers have been found in "tent cities" reminiscent of the dustbowl camps of the 1930s. As reports from throughout the midwest indicate, fewer workers now seem attracted to this southern quest as the discouraging news of their friends and family members filters back. For workers who are in their mid-30s or older, there is nowhere to go. As a private demographic forecaster for Southwestern Bell Telephone, Kara Danter, put it, "The word has finally made its way into the national consciousness that Texas is not immune to economic downturn" (Reinhold, 1985). Indeed, Oklahoma and Wyoming lost people in 1984 and 1985, while growth in states like Colorado and Louisiana was minuscule.

With migration an unattractive option for the new unemployed, the collective, long-term, and more militant choice has become the primary option left if workers are to hold out any hope for maintaining their previous way of life. These campaigns, often waged under a coalition banner of an "unemployed council," have focused on four issues:

(a) legislation for job training and community economic revitalization;
(b) utility-rate freezes;
(c) antiforeclosure campaigns;
(d) taking over and restructuring previous place of employment.

The last economic program is the most complex and yet will receive the least attention here because other works more fully address the variety of approaches deindustrialized workers can use to keep their plants open (Carnoy and Shearer, 1980). What these works detail are the considerable risks, financial packages, and political benefits and costs to workers and their communities in attempting plant takeovers. As is now well known, for every well-publicized bailout of a major firm (such as in the Wheeling, West Virginia steel yards) there are three to four attempted takeovers that do not succeed—the cost of recapitalization is seen as too high and the likelihood of profitability too low to make the ventures worthwhile. (There are also considerable arguments over the causes for costs being so great, most often centering on previous management decisions to not reinvest annually in modest capital improvements so that quarterly profit margins were kept high. Likewise, parent firms and banks—not the workers themselves—have been the stumbling blocks when profit returns have been forecast as too low. These arguments have been detailed in Bluestone and Harrison's *Deindustrialization* and Carnoy and Shearer's *Economic Democracy.* They need to be read by anyone working with organizations opting for this possible solution to unemployment problems.) Anyone considering this option of economic plant revitalization will need serious financial and legal advice on the pitfalls such an undertaking can create.

Such long-term efforts are usually engaged in by a range of high-powered organizations, ranging from labor unions to churches to local banks. While they have received much national publicity, they will take years of effort (Carnoy and Shearer, 1980). In the meantime, unemployed councils, like the councils of the 1930s, engage in both concrete service needs of their membership and short-term organizing campaigns capable of generating enough momentum to keep people's expectations for change alive.

The services offered by the Warren County (Penn.) Unemployed Council are prototypical of what unemployed councils offer their membership. Working out of a "no-frills" business office in downtown Warren (where the rent has been paid through a local Episcopal Church grant), the council starts with a standard "information and referral service"—"keeping track of all the agencies that can help provide the essentials of living, such as food, fuel, mortgage, and medical help" (National Unemployed News, 1984 is a good resource guide for unemployed workers' groups). Members know which doctors will take Medicaid, where foodbanks are located, and learn how to apply for various entitlement programs. Often getting this information from fellow unemployed victims who have been in the council for a while, they are also encouraged to take any job they can find, even part-time or odd jobs. Art Seger, a formerly unemployed worker and president of the council said, "We encourage people to work part-time, accept odd jobs, or any job at all to help themselves. We have referrals—that part-time work that [Public] Job Services doesn't do. We serve as a convenient place for employers to list those openings. We also help the Salvation Army with distribution and other heavy work. . . It's important for people to keep busy" (Hornblum, 1985).

What differentiates this firm commitment to the psychological value in work from the conservative belief in the work ethic itself is the council's equally strong political conviction that such jobs will not be enough to help their members regain their past economic and social circumstances. Their direct-service counseling is always balanced with a request to get members involved in local campaigns of a more political nature. Some involve legislative demands related to keeping local industry from moving, creating a "bill of necessities for the unemployed" for civic, church, and political groups to endorse, and other lobbying efforts related to extending unemployment benefits, increasing welfare grants, and so on. Other campaigns have a more direct action focus. The most popular of those have been the utility-rate campaigns; the most militant are the antiforeclosure struggles.

According to activists, utility-rate campaigns are popular because of the accessibility of the target and the commonly held dislike of utility companies throughout the population. Almost all state and large municipal utility services have public commissions regulating them. Such commissions must hold regular hearings open to the public, which makes such meetings handy targets around which to organize. Groups in Ohio, Pennsylvania, and Alabama used these meetings as their focus to attract attention to the plight of the unemployed. "There is nothing as powerful as a few tearful mothers relating their horror stories that happened to them and their children in the dead of winter," said one activist. "First, they're telling the truth. The media gets a good story for the late news, and our bill gets a wide hearing. No one *loves* utility rates, no matter how rich they are, so we gain access to people we normally can't reach."

These campaigns, focusing on the commission meetings to mobilize support, usually make two demands: an end to shutoffs of electricity and gas between November 1st and April 1st; and a flat rate for poor people—called "life-line rates"—that specifically lowers rates for qualified poor people. Both campaigns depend on accurate data to legitimate these demands.

Unemployed councils in the Birmingham area have used these hotlines to document their cutoff claims. Sandra Poole, a social worker for the Salvation Army, used the agency's data to inform the Birmingham Utility Commission that in one winter month alone utility requests had risen $22,000—a sum her agency could not provide (Barber, 1985). A Pittsburgh group demonstrated that cutoff rates doubled in the two months previous to the shutoff moratorium that exists in Pennsylvania. (Most states do not have provisions for any moratorium.) The campaign works off the two-pronged tactic of demonstrating the needs of the poor and the indifference of the utility to increase popular support for the winter moratorium. Ohio, Pennsylvania, New York, and Vermont have passed such legislation; 12 other states, all with active councils lobbying for the effort, are considering them.

The commissions themselves are pushed to lower rates for the poor. Here the councils use the difference in percentages of monthly income paid by the poor as opposed to average utility users. The average user pays 5%; the poor between 20% and 40% (National Unemployed News, 1984: 2). This statistic, when coupled with the consistent pressure of council-organized commission public hearings, led the Ohio Utility Commission to pass a life-line rate for all qualified poor. This law set a far lower, 10% of income rate as the amount the poor had to pay each month in order to receive electricity and gas through the winter months. The difference in revenues would then be paid partially through increased payments by the poor in the less costly summer months and through state subsidies.

These campaigns have had modest success in states across the country. They draw on traditional tactics of moral indignity, personal suffering, and concrete solutions to build their case against a target many are willing to join within a coalition of support. The techniques of coalition building and legislative advocacy are as traditional as any to be found in the community-organizing literature (Burghardt, 1982: chap. 7). However, the antiforeclosure campaigns are quite different, creating a degree of intensity not seen recently in most American organizing efforts.

The reasons for such passion are obvious: they relate to property, home, and community in both literal and symbolic ways that strike deeply within the American psyche. Some of our most enduring myths surround beliefs of a person's right to own land, and that such ownership bestowed on an individual the rights and privileges to be thought of as equal to any other. "A man's home is his castle" was a statement of pride that however meager one's surroundings, if he or she owned them, they deserved equality with others far richer. The dreadful suicides and homicides of recent years in the agricultural midwest have been about these foreclosures and the power of these dreams that, once altered, affect an entire way of life. The economic crisis of the last decade has dictated that such foreclosures will occur, but the heartbreak and anger that have surfaced in response suggests that the inevitability of all the new unemployed losing their homes is not as certain.

Movies like *Country* and *The River* demonstrated, in bits and pieces, how people have been groping to find collective solutions to problems they never thought could happen—the loss of their property. But in 1984 the Philadelphia Unemployment Project led a more concerted antiforeclosure effort that created an alternative that actually suggests clearly how people can enact laws that make foreclosure far less likely in the future.

The nation's first state-financed mortgage/assistance program was passed in 1984. However, the campaign for foreclosure relief began in mid-1982 in Pittsburgh and Philadelphia in a fashion no less dramatic than found on film. In Pittsburgh, 65 Mon Valley Unemployed Council members attended a sheriff's auction of area homes of unemployed people. Instead of paper markers signifying bids, the members flew cardboard vultures across the room. The auction was peppered with boos and chants, "No jobs, no sales!" and penny bids from the angry members. Instead of housing sales that day, five families won postponement on their homes being sold. Two nights later, the City Council unanimously passed a recommendation to lenders to call a moratorium on foreclosures on the homes of the unemployed "indefinitely."

In Philadelphia, an employed single mother was faced with imminent foreclosure and eviction one month later. But when the sheriff's deputies came to vacate the house, they found it barricaded by 40 people who blocked the porch and front door and marched across the front lawn with signs. The police arrived shortly—and so did about 35 of the woman's neighbors. The police were told to arrest all of them or none. They arrested none. When PUP called the mortgage company, the company was uncooperative. So the demonstrators moved to the company's office. By late afternoon, the woman had an indefinite stay on her foreclosure.

These vignettes are told in detail to demonstrate the tactical militance used to focus attention on the problem of foreclosures. Unlike utilities, there are no commissions that oversee all property transactions, no public hearings announced in a highly accessible manner. It is a much more private but perhaps even more emotional experience between the homeowner, the mortgage company and, eventually, the sheriff's office. Because it speaks directly to property rights—both those of the homeowner *and* the holder of the mortgage who, under the rights of capitalism, deserves payment in full—the issues lead to confrontation because there is no easy middle ground. One feels the right to their home, the other to receive payments for the home. It is thus no simple matter, and in the context of a statewide increase in mortgage foreclosures of over 36% between 1980 and 1982 (26% nationwide), the sparks for serious conflict were increasingly present. In rural counties, the number of foreclosures had increased 200% in four years.

After these ad hoc demonstrations, the council work fell into two categories: research into those companies that initiated foreclosure procedures more rapidly than others, and consistent protest over different families' problems (which helped bring them more lenient payment terms).

While this organizing and advocacy went on, the councils across the state began to draft legislation specifically designed to give wide-scale relief. The groups organized a "Foreclosure Crisis Committee," which, like utility commissions, held hearings across the state to drum up support for the legislation. This helped publicize their cause and helped enlist prominent labor, civic, and religious organizations in the effort. Local and state politicians were invited to do the same; more and more did as they saw communitywide support. Legislation—modeled after a HUD program that had helped people with federal mortgages stave off foreclosures—was introduced to create a loan fund for families who had fallen behind on mortgages "due to circumstances beyond their control" (this was specifically added so it primarily covered homeowners who had lost their jobs due to plant shutdowns). Other provisions included the homeowner "demonstrating a reasonable prospect of resuming full monthly payments within 36 months." The bill created a $25 million fund to provide low-interest loans to residents about to lose their homes. A three-month moratorium on all fore-closures was also added to the bill, with a codicil attached stating this moratorium would be in effect for two years before state review.

Banks and mortgage companies were opposed to the legislation and worked furiously for its defeat. But the consistent grass-roots effort of the councils, especially when joined by powerful allies such as the AFL-CIO and the Pennsylvania Council of Churches, were able to build remarkable support for a bill once considered a lost cause in the legislature. The bill was passed in 1983 and won adequate funding in May 1984.

This struggle has been told in great detail here because it represents many of the trends in organizing witnessed across the country in the 1980s: direct services to sustain members, coalition building with more powerful allies, legislative advocacy, and, perhaps most surprising, a well-orchestrated use of militance and moral outrage to solidify their cause. The Pennsylvania foreclosure moratorium campaign was two-and-a-half years in the making, and its success occurred through a tremendous amount of hard work at the grass-roots level, research, and outreach to other allies to make it a success. By joining their picketing and sit-ins with clear documentation of the mortgage companies' practices, they joined their call for justice among beleaguered homeowners with a picture of greedy profiteers. They didn't fight against property rights, but used others' belief in them as they compared others' drive for profits. This careful selection of mortgage companies left the picture of justice and fairness clearly on the side of the unemployed. Likewise, they did not begin their foreclosure hearings around the state until they had legislation available that was based on extant federal laws. Such previously used legislation heightened the credibility of the hearings, and gave the unemployed council activists easier entree to established groups who otherwise might have viewed their efforts as fringe activity.

But perhaps most important was the consistent reliance on, and mobilization of, unemployed people themselves to take part in these efforts. As can be seen in other successful advocacy efforts in the 1980s (such as with the disabled in their fight for Independent Living Centers—see chap. 6), organizers knew they would not expect consistent numbers to turn out and help in their efforts if direct services—information and referral, job placement, etc.— were not part of what they offered the new unemployed. It was the respect of their immediate concerns—given without demands for other levels of activism—that seems to have led a significant percentage of new unemployed to become active in utility rate and foreclosure campaigns. Of course, their conditions were not as perilous as those of the homeless and hungry. Many had the skills and time to participate that other issues' constituencies did not. Future organizing efforts will have to utilize similar services if they expect to mobilize as effectively as they did in Pennsylvania.

Of course, the successful legislation in Pennsylvania, like the number of Independent Living Centers for the disabled, is not enough for all the ills of the group they wish to serve, nor do they reach everyone in need. But their success serves as a clear, concrete reminder that organizing campaigns, even when both militant and an implicit challenge to the rights of property, can succeed when the right strategic elements fall into place. There was no more likelihood of success for the Pennsylvania activists in 1982 than there is in Alabama or Oregon today. By incorporating the right combination of militancy, research, service, moralism, and savvy legislative skills, all within a statewide context of widespread unemployment and uncertain futures for many once-solid citizens, these unemployed councils developed a model that can be used elsewhere. Those elements are: (1) *looking after the concrete concerns and psychological needs of their membership*—part-time work and referrals on entitlements were always a part of these councils' activities; (2) *multi-issue campaigns.* The long-term concern surrounding employment was addressed by not only looking for jobs and new industries but by making the wider public aware of the new unemployed's plight through the utility rate and foreclosure campaigns, support for expanded health insurance, fighting for the extension of unemployed benefits, and so on. Each campaign had an "unemployed bill of rights," in which mention was made of other campaigns. The inevitable lull as one issue developed in different stages allowed campaigns to merge and help support each other in coalition efforts. The media might grow tired of rate campaigns, but foreclosure legislation would become timely. While such bills wound through the legislative process, a demonstration over health insurance cutoffs became topical. In this manner, the coalitional efforts sustained each other by supporting the leading activists of one issue while knowing their own efforts would garner equivalent support later on. The coalitional efforts took on a sustaining quality, rather than leading up to the all-too-familiar infighting in other alliances. (3) *Militancy was buttressed with facts, and facts were given life through direct action.* These groups didn't shy away from militance and the threat of arrest, but they chose their issues and their targets carefully, using sustainable data and not just "justice" to bolster their actions. Likewise, data were not left to the often dusty corridors of legislative halls, either. The foreclosure moratorium joined legislative acumen with pickets and emotional testimonials, the latter actions being controlled far more by the grass roots' activists themselves. In either example, *no one tactic* was allowed to dominate the council's strategy, but a variety seemed to have been used consistently. (4) *No one council was allowed to develop into an all-powerful bureaucratic force capable of smothering other councils' development.* One of the purposes in each campaign, especially the foreclosure campaign, was to build new councils across Pennsylvania. This is not to say older, more established groups weren't more influential; they were, and rightly so. But it is a telling lesson that at the end of this foreclosure campaign there were 12 councils instead of only 2 in the state. By keeping each group scaled down to a size compatible with membership needs for content and control, these groups spoke to the antibureaucratic message that fuels both the left and right as they critique large-scale organizations in the United States.

There is no great likelihood that this organizing activity will be easily replicated in other parts of the country. But these four strategic elements that underpin their efforts are worthy of any group's consideration. For while there is no guarantee of success, the Pennsylvania Unemployed Council's antiforeclosure campaign is a clear indication that hope lies in the strategic utilization of a piece of history that *worked*—and for homeowners in one state, that history worked well.

APPENDIX:
Preplanning Questions

What is the unemployment rate in your area? How long has it been at that level, and is it changing in any one direction?

Of those who are unemployed, how many would be part of the new unemployed—working people with long work histories who find themselves out of work due to plant shutdowns or cutbacks and unable to find equivalent jobs at the same wages.

Does your community have a history of trade unionism? Which unions? What committees have they established to help their unemployed members? Are they engaged in projects to keep or bring industry to the area?

What economic development plans are there in the city, county, or region? Locate forecasts on future trends. Which groups—unions, churches, civic associations—are involved? Have they prepared a prospectus for any industry? What are their *specific* suggestions regarding the currently unemployed population?

Building an Unemployed Council[1]
—Locate interested people to form a planning committee—how broad a cross-section of the community do they represent?
—What service training is needed? How many programs exist in your area that are of interest to your membership? Work to establish good relations with other groups, public and private, involved in entitlement work.

Building a Campaign
—Establish credibility through research. Use data from other programs, hotlines, and official records (including sheriff's auctions and notices of foreclosure) to choose your initial campaign.
—Include in all interviews questions about political issues and possible organizing campaigns. Watch to see how people react to each issue.
—Locate other unemployed councils in the state and region. Contact the National Unemployed Council—116 South 7th Street, Suite 610, Phila., PA 19106. They have a list of all current unemployed councils.

Strategic Questions
—What percentage of unemployed will be part of the council leadership? A Majority? Plurality? Less?
—What degree of militance is acceptable to the membership?
—What blend of legislative activity and grass-roots mobilization will the council strive for? Too much lobbying risks a loss of grass-roots activism; too little runs the danger of irrelevance in these conservative times.
—What targets seem most likely to respond to a grass-roots campaign? Are the utility companies burdened with an especially bad reputation? Are there politicians up for reelection who are running important legislative committees? Are there community traditions of self-reliance you can tap effectively?

NOTE

1. The preplanning suggestions for Food Resource Centers regarding space, membership composition, etc., can be followed here as well. See Chapter 3.

Chapter 8

FROM UNDER THE SAFETY NET TO EMPOWERMENT:
New Organizational and Practice Directions for the 1990s

There are two primary messages of this book. The first is that new and intensified forms of poverty are affecting an expanding pool of Americans. Single room occupancy (SRO) hotels and tenement dwellings were often considered substandard forms of housing in the late 1960s and early 1970s. Today, however, such housing is increasingly unavailable to low-income citizens. Consequently, the housing crisis has become the homelessness crisis and S.R.O.s are being replaced by cardboard boxes on city street corners. Americans who rely on food stamps to meet their nutritional or dietary needs simply can no longer make it on their allowance. Report after report has indicated that a swelling epidemic of hunger is striking at a cross-section of Americans.

This comes as no surprise to service workers who encounter unemployed steel workers in Mon Valley or folks on fixed incomes in urban areas who have husbanded their scarce resources and still exhausted their food stamps by the second or third week of the month. Food stamps, which were expected to resolve hunger in America during the 1960s and 1970s are effectively being replaced by private soup kitchens and food pantries. Clearly, the locus of responsibility for these services is rapidly being shifted from the public to the private sector. In effect, if sufficient housing or food stamps are unavailable to low- and moderate-income citizens then private groups or individuals at risk are expected by default independently to resolve these crises. This type of response to personal and communal crises is reminiscent of the early 1930s. At that time both churches and the individual were expected independently to resolve the communal and personal disruptions (loss of jobs, housing, hunger, etc.) of the Great Depression. Current trends indicate that social services are being *reprivatized.*

In a related way, groups of citizens who have been defined as the "worthy poor" are also witnessing an intensified attack upon their standard of living. Physically disabled citizens, the elderly and recently unemployed have all been targeted for entitlement cutbacks during the 1980s. More specifically, it was proposed that social-security payments be scaled back over time by placing a cap on cost-of-living adjustments (C.O.L.A.) for inflation. Additionally, approximately a half-million physically disabled citizens receiving S.S.D.I. benefits were declared ineligible at the conclusion of an administrative-review process. Finally, there was an effort to reduce the period that recently unemployed citizens are eligible for unemployment benefits. Each of these proposals and initiatives effectively suggested that the elderly, physically disabled, and recently unemployed, would no longer be guaranteed even the minimal economic supports that until recently had been available. This shift in public policy has had a profound impact upon the content and quality of life of these groups of citizens.

Another group that has been further marginalized during this period is poor black female-headed families. Some of these families rely on Aid for Families with Dependent Children benefits (A.F.D.C.). These benefits, however, have at best increased modestly while expenses during the past decade have soared. Just as important, stepped-up attacks on welfare have been initiated and, consequently, more stringent application and reapplication procedures have been legislated. These application procedures have frequently functioned to delay and deny benefits to families in economic crisis.

There has been a recent effort to move A.F.D.C. beneficiaries into the job market through work-fare programs. However, these programs do not contain either the incentives (adequate wages, potential for upward mobility, skill development) or supports (child care) to affect substantial movement into the job market. Too often, these programs have been used to harass A.F.D.C. beneficiaries and remove them from the rolls for noncompliance. It is most unfortunate that job programs having the potential of positively transforming the lives of welfare beneficiaries and their families are structured not to affect such change but rather to further regulate and destabilize the existence of this group of citizens. The consequence for A.F.D.C. families is that they have been placed in the no-win situation of being forced to participate in dead-end job programs while concurrently being expected to progress toward independence and self-sufficiency. This is but one of the contradictory tendencies embedded within the debate on welfare programs that on the one hand rhetorically argues for independence and on the other structurally denies beneficiaries the opportunity to progress toward self-sufficiency.

A question that must be asked is why the circumstance of so many citizens has deteriorated during the past decade. Clearly, the policies of the Reagan Administration are the most apparent explanation for the proliferation of homelessness and hunger as well as the increased vulnerability of other groups of citizens (elderly, physically disabled, and new unemployed). Recent budget cutbacks have adversely affected both the standard of living and security of a range of vulnerable groups. However, more fundamental economic and social forces than mere presidential fiat have forced a reduction in the base income of American citizens.

As was explained in the first chapter, due to a crisis in capital accumulation American workers in general have been forced to accept substantially reduced wages and benefits in order to cut production costs. As the wages in the private sector have been reduced, there has been a concurrent effort to depress the social wages or level of entitlement for certain nonworking segments of the American population. It has been suggested that the reduction of labor-market wages had to affect social wage reductions (overtime) if the incentives of the market place or doctrine of less eligibility was to be preserved (Fabricant, 1985: 389-395). Simply put, such entitlement reductions are expected to assure that a sufficient number of laborers will choose work over welfare. The dynamics of this policy of service retrenchment also reflect the neoconservative perspective that social-service investments drain away much needed capital from private investments. For them increased spending in this area was primarily responsible for the decline of the economy and the subsequent fiscal crisis. It was on this basis that policies were implemented that redistributed monies from social services (budget cuts, restricted eligibility, etc.) to the private sector (tax cuts). It is clear that social wage or entitlement reductions are associated with trends in the larger economy. These policy choices have served to destabilize further the circumstance of many groups of citizens receiving various forms of entitlement assistance.

Cuts in social services are occurring at a time when need continues to expand. The increased levels of unemployment and reduced wages have created many service needs among these new yet potentially chronically unemployed and underemployed citizens. Recent data suggest that the stress of unemployment is strongly associated with acts of violence toward self and others. Increased drug taking and alcoholism are also associated with unemployment. Minority youth may never experience the labor market in this economic climate. Recent estimates indicate that depending upon the urban area, between 50% and 90% of minority youth are unemployed (Hopper and Hamberg, 1985; Fabricant and Kelly, 1986). Additionally, the number of single adolescent women bearing children is increasing, especially among whites. Finally, decisions by state governments to release mental patients into the community without adequate support services represents yet another area of unmet need. These factors have combined to create new populations that are effectively "falling below the safety net" (Hopper and Hamberg, 1985).

In general, social-service agencies are unable to meet the new and intensified forms of need that are affecting those citizens who are falling below the safety net. To begin with, the paperwork and regulations that increasingly define social-service work hinder the agencies' capacity to respond immediately and appropriately to a hungry, homeless, or recently unemployed citizen (Fabricant, 1986). Instead, the welter of rules and stream of paper are likely to delay significantly the delivery of needed services. Too often public agencies fail to intervene on the day such need is identified and instead ask citizens to return on subsequent work days. Such a judgment effectively forces people to remain in their already dire circumstances and risk rapid destabilization, i.e., physical illness, crime on the streets, emotional deterioration, eviction, or mortgage foreclosure.

Second, these new forms of need frequently no longer fit within the programmatic categories that have been developed by the government. For instance, there are no procedures or services for elderly or recently unemployed citizens who have exhausted their monthly allocation of food stamps other than to refer them to already overwhelmed and understaffed soup kitchens. Similarly, A.F.D.C. recipients who have been evicted are often left little option but to spend their monthly checks on a cheap motel room and once their benefits are exhausted to rely upon friends or relatives for shelter. There are few programs available to A.F.D.C. recipients that provide the necessary income supports to locate permanent housing. Citizens with multiple needs such as the physically disabled homeless are particularly underserved. Again, this group falls outside of certain categorical program definitions and consequently few services exist to meet daily necessities.

Agencies are also constrained by the fiscal limitations of recent years. Clearly, the resources necessary to meet basic needs (food, housing, shelter, etc.) are increasingly unavailable. As has already been noted, entitlement benefits available from programs as otherwise disparate as Social Security and A.F.D.C. share a diminished capacity to meet needs as basic as rent. Just as important, many of these programs are greatly understaffed and consequently assign little value to follow-up activity. Therefore, workers are expected to process a substantial volume of clients but not to address the basic inadequacy of their clients' fixed income or their follow-up needs.

Finally, the few and scattered services that have recently been organized to meet the needs of citizens falling below the safety net often have more symbolic than real value. Shelters are temporary residences that do not address permanent housing needs; soup lines and food pantries are stop-gap measures that usually offer a couple of meals a week but cannot meet the basic dietary needs of citizens; work-fare programs do not lead to permanent jobs for A.F.D.C. beneficiaries and the few job programs available to the recently unemployed do not allow them to duplicate their former earning power or compete in regional labor markets. Relatedly, such programs are scarce commodities and, consequently, can only address a fraction of the need of the homeless, hungry, or recently unemployed. These programs then are incapable of addressing either the short- or long-term needs of these citizens.

The fiscal crisis then has produced new and intensified areas of need and a service system that is unprepared to meet these new demands. The distinctive characteristic of each of the populations discussed in this book is an intensified daily struggle to survive. Given the diminished role of the state and the survival problems experienced by these groups, organizational structures and practice approaches will have to be recreated to meet the new service demands of the late 1980s and 1990s. The rest of this chapter will develop a preliminary sketch of a multifaceted practice and organizational context that is most effective in meeting the needs of these groups of citizens.

The common underpinnings of approaches that have been tested and proven effective will provide the basis for the discussion. We have developed this formulation from the analyses in the preceding six chapters. The second message of this book is that creative service and advocacy approaches have begun to emerge out of the struggle to secure better services and rights for these groups. Indeed, while *empowerment* is a term used in the literature with such ease as to lose its meaning, we will argue that much of what occurs "under the safety net" is genuinely empowering for worker and citizen alike.

LESSONS OF RECENT STRUGGLES

The empowerment process described in this book has evolved out of the contradictory tendencies service workers confront in their practice. Unlike the 1960s, there are few illusions about economic and social limitations imposed by the larger social order. A service worker could work 24 hours a day, 7 days a week, and not help enough. Many clients may struggle valiantly and still be able to do little more than reach a modest level of subsistence through underemployment and reduced social-wage benefits.

Given this reality, all forms of successful individual advocacy, organizational development, and coalition building have contributed to a critically conscious dynamic of responding to immediate need while educating and training for long-term social awareness and change. Whether disabled activist or hunger advocate, the combination of working on specific issues while formulating an active awareness of problems based in the larger political economy seems most effective as groups move *between* individual concerns and systemic problems. In terms of method, this has meant a move toward an updated form of generic work. No single method—be it casework or community organization—is unilaterally effective today. One may be trained in a method of choice, but working under the safety net retrains the case worker to connect his or her case advocacy or information and referral skills to problems of the larger social order. In turn, the community practitioner's strategic skills are refined to work on the immediate needs of clients too desperate to look beyond questions of survival. Neither can be effective without these added skill areas. Both need the *social vision* of long-term empowerment if they are to struggle within the limitation of this work without succumbing to cynical fatalism.

We will look at this social vision later. It is sufficient to note at this point in the analysis that much of what follows attempts to incorporate this empowering vision into the daily tasks of working beneath the safety net.

As this book has indicated repeatedly, the worker begins with the immediate crisis or problem experienced by economically vulnerable citizens. Little trust can be established between worker and citizen if primary attention is not paid to the unemployed worker's fear of mortgage foreclosure, the homeless person's panic about returning to the street, the elderly citizen's physical deterioration due to malnutrition, or the physically disabled individual's loss of entitlement benefits. The worker must adhere to one of the most fundamental tenets of the social work profession by remaining *client centered*. In effect, the problems identified by these citizens as primary must be assigned equal value by the worker. If the worker fails to address these real threats to the economic and physical well-being of their clients, then there will be little, if any, opportunity to establish an ongoing relationship. Additionally, the worker must, *to the extent possible,* address these problems as crises that require immediate and urgent attention. To the extent that there is a delayed response, the problem will in all probability become increasingly unmanageable and the worker will lose legitimacy. This book has repeatedly indicated that a critical prerequisite for effective agency-based practice with citizens falling under the safety net is the development of a sensibility that remains attuned to particular crises and needs. Only this sensibility in combination with a commitment toward developing a rapid plan of action offer the potential for establishing strong bonds with citizens who are falling under the safety net.

Clearly, the factors that are destabilizing the circumstance of the recently unemployed worker, elderly, physically disabled, or poor black female-headed families are located not in the individual but the larger social environment. Consequently, if the circumstance of the homeless, hungry, or physically disabled is to improve the immediate struggles of these individual citizens must first be addressed while also attempting to show how their problems are externally located in the political economy. This has happened most often after initial support is given and the organization itself is connected to wider struggles. If for instance, one is helping a few homeless individuals while the agency is simultaneously engaged in fighting for more housing through an antigentrification campaign, that organizing can be organically linked to individual problems in a clear and direct manner. As we found, the activism involved in this struggle serves the additional purpose of helping once-isolated individuals to externalize much of their condition. Without fostering a false determinism—people on the streets will have individual problems too—this organic connection between individual or group issues and societal conditions exemplifies the essence of empowerment sought by so many human-service workers. Organizations and service formulations that have highlighted these interrelationships are particularly apparent in the areas of homelessness, hunger, and physical disability.

Obviously, a variety of tensions will be experienced by workers who attempt to develop practice formulations that struggle to meet the short- and long-term needs of citizens who are falling under the safety net. To begin with, social-service workers will often have to balance paperwork and other demands of particular agencies against the specific and immediate crises of clients. Additionally, the resolution of individual problems that require substantial resources such as housing, shelter, food, or income will be stymied by an environment that is reducing such options. Often it will be difficult to sort out where to begin when citizens come in with multiple problems that appear to be equally compelling. Internal-agency supports that are often critical to enabling workers to develop their emergent craft such as peer supports, in-house training, salary increases, and promotions may be scarce. Activists working under the safety net often established mutual aid/support groups to help deal with these complex issues. Sometimes the groups were little more than "brown-bag lunches" where people shared weekly lessons and aired frustrations in a supportive environment. Often times study groups emerged to examine social policy issues more fully. This enabled workers to use learning as a healthy process that placed them inside an historical process that was larger, more powerful, and more exciting than simple routines of stress-inducing activism. Utilization of history and economic policy had the restorative effect of reminding workers of the social vision underpinning the daily fights for help and survival—a social vision that they were actively maintaining and recreating.

This social vision can create frustrations and often did for activists in all arenas of work. The pull toward grander formulations will be substantial. However, given present economic trends only modest initiatives will provide the building blocks necessary to create the basis for broader and more sweeping challenges of present social policies. Groups that failed often engaged in larger challenges that initially appeared more exciting, but without proper support led to a series of failures and ultimately the withdrawal of involved workers from future struggles. Successful struggles engaged the issue(s) differently. For example, the successful mortgage-foreclosure fights of the Philadelphia Unemployment Project developed out of individual efforts to stave off foreclosure, group or community education, and legislative planning. People beneath the safety net must make careful choices during this period about the actions to organize or support.

As the P.U.P. example underscores, however, it is important to remember that workers with this vision can engage in important struggles with economically vulnerable groups of citizens and win. For instance, a range of social-service workers aligned with the elderly during the 1980s and preserved most of the social-security benefits that were at risk. At a local level, groups of concerned private citizens, social-service workers, and physically disabled people have contributed to the creation of independent-living programs and pressured officials to improve access to public buildings and transportation centers. Advocates across the country in concert with currently and formerly homeless citizens have contributed to the development of shelters, housing, and supportive-living programs. A number of food pantries and soup kitchens have emerged during the past five years because of the effective advocacy of social-service workers, clergy, and the hungry.

Clearly, each of these victories is modest. They have not solved the problems of the homeless, hungry, recently unemployed, elderly, or physically disabled. At best, many of these efforts have been defensive maneuvers intended to preserve entitlement programs or economic rights that are under attack. Each of these victories shares the common ground of beginning with those issues that are most central to the lives of affected populations. It is only by first preserving peoples' right to survive (shelters and food pantries) and hard-won economic rights (S.S.D.I., Social Security, and unemployment insurance) that the groundwork can be laid for advancing definitions of economic entitlement.

These victories in concert with individual efforts of empowerment then have the potential of transforming the struggles of these groups of citizens from a defensive to aggressive posture. The interrelationship between these two levels of intervention breaks down into the following categories of intervention: (1) case-empowerment advocacy; (2) class advocacy, and (3) program development/coalition building. These approaches use distinctive professional skills but are united by a clear social vision that lifts these efforts into an ongoing empowerment process. Service workers have made a positive difference in the lives of citizens falling under the safety net when they have chosen to participate in a change process that by definition requires substantial struggle. The elements of this practice approach will be sketched in the next section of the chapter.

PRACTICE UNDER THE SAFETY NET

CASE-EMPOWERMENT ADVOCACY

We have called the individual-case efforts of practitioners working beneath the safety net "case-empowerment advocacy" because advocacy has too limited a definition for the kind of individual work most effective in the 1980s. As we suggested earlier in this chapter, citizens in need today require various forms of immediate assistance such as help in negotiating increasingly bureaucratized agency structures. They also require ongoing educational efforts and support around systemic issues if they are to prepare for the long-term struggles surrounding basic survival needs. This joint effort contains the empowerment dynamics sought by activists today.

A practitioner responding to an individual's immediate survival needs must have a knowledge of (1) client, (2) community resources, and (3) other social-service agencies.

At the earliest stages of initial contact, the advocate must collect certain pertinent information. Prior to engaging in any type of advocacy, the provider must (1) assess or diagnose the problem; (2) understand the client's employment, psychological background, and so on, to determine eligibility for various forms of entitlement; (3) clarify recent experiences with entitlement workers or agencies; and (4) identify other community or familial resources that have historically been available. Once this information has been gathered, the advocate can then attempt to assure that appropriate and timely emergency assistance is provided, i.e., food, shelter, heating allowance, and the like.

It is also the job of the advocate to know both the law and the citizens' circumstances prior to engaging entitlement officials. The advocate then must be prepared to present a strong case and engage the department as a potential adversary. If the request for emergency assistance is denied, legal services or other public-interest lawyers must be contacted to explore the possibilities for an appeal.

These forms of emergency assistance, however, are incapable of sustaining a person indefinitely. The generally more lengthy process of obtaining permanent forms of assistance needs to be entered into concurrently. Again, the advocate must identify the entitlement that most closely approximates the person's circumstance. For instance, a citizen with a physical or emotional disability may be eligible for SSI or SSDI, a female-headed family may be eligible for A.F.D.C., etc. The advocate can then enable the citizen to negotiate the service bureaucracy by helping explain laws, fill out paperwork, engage or work around service personnel, and so on.

Assuming that emergency and permanent assistance are eventually obtained, the advocate may also participate in a search for permanent housing, a job, or other discrete services. Again, formal agency and informal community contacts can provide critical leads during the course of this process. Consequently, the worker should maintain an ongoing list of community people and agency personnel who are sympathetic and connected to such resources.

The process of stabilization also requires that the person in need not become increasingly dependent upon the scarce time and resources of the advocates, but rather they be trained to negotiate independently the welfare system. Such empowerment training must be built into the ongoing work of the advocate (i.e., pointing out pertinent laws, techniques, sympathetic workers, etc.) as the bureaucracy is being negotiated. Otherwise, the case load(s) can only swell as both new and old contacts continue to require a full range of services. Another important mechanism that can contribute to the process of stabilization is the development of citizen support groups. The support group can function as a vehicle that enables the very poor to work with each other during their (1) emotional transitions, (2) searches for housing, jobs, food, etc., (3) struggles with children, shelter living, or life on the street, and (4) efforts to develop an understanding of external factors affecting their lives. Given the isolated circumstance of these economically vulnerable citizens it is critical that approaches be developed that address their communal needs. Consequently, although the case-empowerment advocate's primary role at this time is to secure stabilizing service for the very poor, it is only through the development of secondary advocacy services that emphasize self-reliance and group (or communal) supports that the initial gains of stabilization are likely to be sustained and deepened.

It is very important to note that each of the activities that have been described under the general heading of case-empowerment advocacy has a "triage"-like quality. In effect, there simply is not a sufficient amount of shelter beds, jobs, housing, or food programs to meet the immediate needs of all citizens who are falling under the safety nets. Second, grant levels for permanent entitlements (G.A., A.F.D.C., S.S.D.I.) are increasingly incapable of meeting these groups of citizens' fundamental needs. Undoubtedly, the gap between the needs of low-income citizens and available resources has been widening.

This crisis for practitioners developed the ironic opportunity of creativity utilizing these individual cases to build toward the next level of empowerment. By closely linking their individual cases to class advocacy designed to affect a substantial investment in entitlements and services, these activists have found a ready connection between once-isolating work and larger actions that have the potential of helping to sustain people over long periods of time.

CLASS ADVOCACY AND HEIGHTENED VISIBILITY OF THE PROBLEM

In general, as long as a social problem is defined as being of only modest proportions and isolated (or located in particular individuals and communities) it will remain invisible. Part of the task of the advocate has been to move the problem from invisibility to visibility by: (1) documenting the substantial and growing size of the homeless, hungry, etc.; (2) contesting what are generally modest public-sector estimates of the problem; (3) associating homelessness, job loss, hunger, etc. with more general trends in the economy; and (4) identifying the inadequacy of available services. The class advocate's battles need to be waged on at least two fronts. The advocate's earlier individualized contact with the bureaucracy or public sector was generally adversarial. It therefore helped dramatize the inadequacy of state policies and proposed resources allocations. (An example of this is not allowing the state to redefine ketchup into a vegetable.) This activity must also, if necessary, underscore the indifference of state officials to the survival needs of citizens falling under the safety net. Clearly, the state has an investment in minimizing both the size of the problem and its resource allocation given the competing demands on its scarce dollars during a period of fiscal austerity.

The other front is intended to penetrate the barriers that have been erected by some people and communities to deny the existence of these problems. These barriers are a product of the fundamental fears associated with homelessness, hunger, or job loss (downward mobility, physical differences, and so on). In the end, however, these "insulating mechanisms" marginalize social problems and render them invisible. There are essentially three types of class-advocacy tactics available to the practitioner that have had the potential of (a) heightening the visibility of the problem (b) dramatizing the inadequate response of the state and (c) forging new alliances across communities. For the purpose of this discussion, these approaches will be classified and labeled as legal, symbolic, and militant.

Perhaps the most popular form of class advocacy currently being utilized in behalf of the very poor is litigation. Various cases have been brought before the courts that include, but are not limited to, right to shelter, restoration of S.S.D.I. allowances, making public buildings accessible to the physically disabled, and extensions of food allowances. Many of these cases were initially handled by advocates who were attempting to secure various forms of assistance for their individual clients. These applications for assistance were denied. Subsequent appeals of these decisions through administrative and legal forums by lawyers have often strengthened the citizens' rights to particular services (Burghardt, 1986).

Legal approaches, however, are both lengthy and can never hope to satisfy the universe of needs of these people. Consequently, other tactics often have been used concurrently that vividly symbolize the policies of the public sector and the consequent circumstance of citizens who are falling under the safety net. An approach that has satisfied these criteria is the development of tent cities of the homeless in front of either city or state government offices. Rallies featuring very poor citizens as speakers also fit within this categorical heading. Other tactics have been utilized by the physically disabled to dramatize their lack of access to public-transportation facilities. These tactics handled with adroitness and good timing increase public pressure and help marshall support for those once assumed invisible or without need.

Militancy generally requires that advocates disobey laws in their pursuit of adequate and appropriate services. For instance, civil disobedience at welfare offices has been an appropriate tactic when homeless individuals and families applied for emergency assistance, were denied, and left no other option but the streets. An alternative approach has been to "squat" in an abandoned public or private building.

Certain prerequisites underpin the use of these broader approaches. To move the social problem to a higher level of visibility, the media must be involved in covering the story. Consequently, some advocates must reach out to cultivate and maintain contact with appropriate reporters and editors. Second, class-advocacy activities require the involvement of the affected groups of citizens. This is the essence of moving empowerment from an abstract to an active reality. Such involvement, however, must be preceded by a clear explanation of the potential costs and benefits to these vulnerable citizens when militancy is planned. It is particularly critical that the types of punishment, harassment, etc., that they may encounter, be clarified. These citizens being given enough information to make an informed decision about their involvement is also part of an empowerment process. This is a basic obligation of the advocate given the relative vulnerability of this group of citizens.

Working with individuals, developing networks, and engaging in wide-scale activity is hard work. In almost all of the cases we examined, new programs and broader coalitions have emerged through these forms of advocacy.

NEW PROGRAMS IN ESTABLISHED AGENCIES

The 1980s has witnessed the development of many programs that are specifically designed to address the new circumstance(s) of an agency's traditional clientele. For instance, many mental-health agencies have developed outreach programs that are intended to assess the needs of homeless people and provide certain critical services on the streets. Churches have become increasingly involved in developing sheltering and food services. Other agencies have established programs that offer supportive nonresidential services to the elderly in their homes.

In general, these programs have evolved out of the case-empowerment advocacy efforts of agency workers. Many proposals for new sheltering and food services have met substantial opposition from city council(s) and local community groups. These programs, however, have emerged throughout the country because agencies have lobbied with legislators, met with supportive community groups, and cultivated the media. These agencies' continued involvement in creating survival programs, despite stiff opposition, can also be traced to activist staff members who frequently and visibly advocate for such services within the umbrella organization.

Survival-service programs are characteristically organized to meet very particular and immediate needs. For example, new health-service programs for the homeless are specifically intended to address disease associated with life on the streets (lice and tuberculosis). New sheltering programs frequently provide little more than a bed to a homeless individual or family. Clearly, these programs are critical to the life-support systems of the very poor. As has been noted, however, these often understaffed programs frequently offer only specialized and temporal solutions to complex and persistent problems. Therefore, these programs need to be expanded to assure basic survival. New programs have emerged that address these citizens' complex and long-term needs.

NEW COMMUNITY-BASED AGENCIES

Examples from the chapter on the homeless, new unemployed, physically disabled, and hungry consistently indicate that new community organizations have emerged during the past decade to advocate on behalf of citizens who are increasingly vulnerable to intensified forms of poverty and emotional deprivation. In general, these organizations have focused on the multiple problems of a particular population, i.e., homeless, physically disabled, hungry. Additionally, these services are targeted at the community in which the organization is located.

The organization's staff by definition engages in generic not specialized forms of social-service practice. Staff members of these organizations develop advocacy, organizing, group work, and community-relations skills. The particularly desperate and complex problems of the new poor require an approach that utilizes case advocacy and group-work skills to stabilize the homeless person's circumstance. Additionally, class advocacy and organizing techniques are expected to help advance this increasingly large group of citizens beyond a subsistence level of income. Just as important, the most visible factors that account for people falling below the safety net, e.g., unemployment, alcoholism, racism, evictions, etc., also require a more general substantive lense.

It has been necessary, given the advocacy role of the worker and agency, that funding sources be committed to the organization's objectives and independence. Sources of revenue have included private foundations, church groups, patrons, and constituent or membership groups. Additionally, limited sources of funding have been available through particular public-sector agencies. In certain instances prerequisites for accepting public-sector funding have been that the contract neither undermine the fundamental objectives of the organization nor exceed 25% of the total agency budget. The latter point has been intended to avoid a growing dependence upon public funds and thus an increasing vulnerability to a particular public agency's directives. This fiscal strategy has been effectively implemented for certain new advocacy organizations serving the physically disabled, homeless, and hungry.

The relatively modest funding base for such work (at least initially) may require a combination of voluntary, part-time, and full-time staff members. Such a mix also has the potential for a rewarding cross-fertilization of ideas and beliefs. This type of organization must be concerned with recruiting volunteers and staff who share a common commitment to social change and advocacy work. The volunteers and part-time staff(s) work schedules will have to be relatively flexible.

These new agencies have almost always developed a support network to help keep them alive. Activists have located churches, community groups, etc., willing to provide critical supports. In some instances, churches have made space available to the provider agency for a minimum rent. Other agencies absorbed copying, printing, postage, or telephone costs. Additionally, network organizations helped locate funding for the particular services being provided by the agency. Finally, each of these organizations were expected to participate either visibly or behind the scenes in advocacy or organizing efforts that challenge the state. In effect, these network organizations provided the new survival agency with certain kinds of legitimation in and outside of the community. Given these service providers' reluctance to confront state policies directly, safety-net activists have developed creative ways for agencies to contribute.[1] These skills must be developed by safety-net activists who are interested in creating independent organizational bases to work with the new poor. This development of network support groups for independent advocacy has been particularly apparent in work with the homeless, hungry, physically disabled, and new unemployed.

Finally, as has already been noted, this type of agency is especially dependent upon the depth of its volunteers' and staff's commitment to survival-service work. Consequently, the agency's authority structure has frequently reflected its particular dependence upon staff and volunteers. The community of workers who effectively are the organization have created a democratic decision-making process to distribute tasks and assign leadership roles. Clearly, this may be a less efficient way of handling internal process, but the dynamics of empowerment have shown how valuable this process is in helping to retain staff and volunteers. Over time, as the organization stabilizes its funding base, advocates may permanently assign staff positions, leadership roles, etc., while the agency continues to struggle to retain its democratic process and integrity. Such an approach assures that the vital connection between community need and service response, which is the life force of the organization, is maintained.

BROAD-BASED COALITIONS

As we have frequently indicated, the increased numbers of economically, emotionally, and physically dislocated citizens and their daily struggle to survive is intimately associated with the crisis in the larger political economy. Such broad-scale dynamics necessitate the development of countervailing coalitions. Only the development of such broad coalitions will provide the basis for future social movements. Activist social-service work under the safety net has contributed to the emergence of coalitions that are confronting both immediate survival issues and the need to advance definitions of human entitlement further.

The coalitions have found that if definitions of need are to shift from survival services (beds, soup lines, etc.) to more advanced definitions of entitlement (housing, minimum income, etc.), then empowerment case and class-advocacy activities with citizens such as the homeless must be organically linked to these larger questions. This can in part be accomplished through class-advocacy efforts that focus on both the need for certain kinds of emergency assistance (a defensive approach inasmuch as it often represents a loss of stability and quality of life for many recipients who are presently receiving public entitlements) and permanent housing, jobs, minimum income, etc. (which aggressively redefines the parameters of the struggle) for all citizens. Additionally, discussions concerning the rationale for, and nature of, economic rights must be incorporated into advocacy work with other service providers and economically vulnerable citizens whenever possible. This has happened most easily in work with the homeless and new unemployed or where stark economic and social forces have directly affected dislocated citizens. Similar discussions have emerged with other groups discussed in this book when activists have made the effort. These and other activities will provide part of the basis for both citizens and service providers to refocus their attention whenever possible on matters that promise more than subsistence services.

Relatedly, these citizens' long-term needs will require that providers and citizens who are falling below the safety net begin to forge alliances with groups that are attempting to expand the pool of available low-income housing (tenants' associations, clergy, independent-housing organizations), increase the number of available jobs (unions, local grass-roots groups), advance the wages of workers (unions), or substantially raise grant levels of entitlements such as A.F.D.C. and G.A. In short, the long-term interests of the homeless, elderly, or physically disabled and service providers working under the safety net dictate that they organize independently and whenever possible, and consolidate with larger organizing efforts because they offer the only opportunity of transforming the political and economic conditions that are daily driving citizens into the most abject poverty witnessed in this country since the Great Depression.

As seen with all of these groups the specific organizing activities may have a local, regional, and national focus, and may utilize differential coalitional structures to heighten its effectiveness. Just as important, the organizing may concentrate on a single area of entitlement, housing, wages, etc., or consider a full panoply of rights that should be available to all citizens. The actions can vary and might include, but would not be limited to, rallies, instructional or educational town meetings, legislative testimony, voter-registration drives, and militant actions. These larger organizing efforts help unify various groups of citizens who are experiencing shared economic decline into a more potent political force that is capable of substantially advancing present definitions of entitlement (for a more detailed account see Fabricant, forthcoming). When such coalition efforts involve campaigns of wide-scale social justice and economic rights the full circle of empowerment is complete. Both citizen and worker who are struggling around individual survival needs can more easily see how their particular condition is part of a larger, more connected struggle for better living and working conditions. In turn, activists can more easily hold onto the personal human dimension that is fundamental to any wider struggle for social justice.

Clearly, the interrelated approaches outlined in this chapter are intended to confront present policy initiatives that deny the magnitude of need and consistently reduce budget allocations to a range of entitlements. This formulation is intended to help create the counterpressure necessary to alter these policy decisions and concomitantly affect a substantial redistribution of resources. This process can help reverse the trends and political climate that are rapidly reducing the funding level and definition of various entitlements. It will also significantly advance the economic rights of all citizens. The movement necessary to affect such change, however, will draw much of its strength from those communities and groups who recognize the connection between their plight and larger social forces. As such, we view this service approach as part of an empowerment process that is structured to reinforce daily the connection between the personal crises of citizens and forces within the larger environment. Through its emphasis on personal support and activism, survival-service agencies and advocates can contribute to the creation of those social movements, which will be pivotal to the long-term economic security of the American poor.

NOTE

1. Such concerns of larger agencies speak to a reality facing safety-net activists. Their work will often be viewed with disfavor by other social and economic groups who have greater power. Therefore, service workers laboring below the safety net must form protective associations or unions. Such associations must be formed to enable workers to regain some measure of control over the quality and content of their work. The practice formulation that has been developed in this discussion, although critical to the survival of an increasing number of citizens, also places the worker at greater risk. The worker is increasingly placed in the position of having to challenge state regulations, laws, and allocations to meet the desperate needs of the new poor. The worker's adversarial role will over time in all probability affect a punitive response on the part of the state. It is therefore important that the workers assure both their integrity and survival by forming associations that both protect their rights as workers and advance their economic rights.

REFERENCES

ASCH, A. and M. ROUSSO (1985) "Therapists with disabilities: theoretical and clinical issues." Psychiatry 8 (February).

ASHBY, J. L., Jr. (1984) "The impact of Medicare prospective payment in large urban areas." District of Columbia Hospital Association J. (September).

BARBER, D. (1985) "Plan sought to help needy pay utility bills." Birmingham News (April 10): A8.

BARRINGER, F. (1983) "The handicapped man." Washington Post (April 12).

BAXTER, E. and K. HOPPER (1981) Private Lives/Public Places: Homeless Adults on the Streets of New York City. New York: Community Service Society.

BAXTER, E. and K. HOPPER (1984) "Shelter and housing for the homeless mentally ill," in R. Lamb (ed.) The Homeless Mentally Ill. Washington, DC: The American Psychiatric Association.

BLUESTONE, B. and B. HARRISON (1982) The Deindustrialization of America. New York: Basic.

BRAND, R. (1985) "Into the bone: the 1986 Reagan health budget." Health-Pac Bulletin (January): 15-17.

BRAVERMAN, H. (1974) Labor and Monopoly Capital. New York: Monthly Review.

BRINKLEY, A. (1983) Voices of Protest. New York: Vintage.

BURESS, C. (1983) "Fending off attacks on rights of disabled: we are still watching." San Francisco Examiner (May 25).

BURGHARDT, S. (1982) The Other Side of Organizing. Cambridge, MA: Schenkman.

BURGHARDT, S. (1982) The Other Side of Organizing. Cambridge, MA: Shenkman.

BURGHARDT, S. (1982) Organizing for Community Action. Beverly Hills, CA: Sage.

BURGHARDT, S. (1983) "The strategic crisis in grass roots organizing." Against the Current (Fall).

BURGHARDT, S. (1986) "Community based practice," in The Encyclopedia of Social Work.

BURT, M. and K. PITTMAN (1985) Testing the Social Safety Net. Washington, DC: Urban Institute.

BUSS, T. R. and F. S. REDBURN, with J. WALDRUM (1983) Mass Unemployment: Plant Closings and Community Mental Health. Beverly Hills, CA: Sage.

California Department of Employment (n.d.) CWEP Evaluation: Interim Report for Period July 1, 1973 to June 30, 1974. Sacramento, CA: Author.

Callahan v. Carey 42582/79 Supreme Court of the State of New York.

CARNOY, M. and D. SHEARER (1980) Economic Democracy. New York: H. C. Sheepe.

CAUDILL, H. M. (1963) Night Comes to the Cumberlands. Boston: Little, Brown.

Coalition on Women and the Budget (1984) "Inequality of sacrifice: the impact of the Reagan budget on women." (unpublished)

COLEMAN, J. (1983) "Diary of a homeless man." New York Magazine (February 21).

Consortium for Citizens with Developmental Disabilities (C.C.D.D.) (1985) Washington, DC: Author.

CRYSTAL, S. (1984) "Homeless men and homeless women: the gender gap." Urban and Social Change Rev. (Summer).

DANZIGER, S. and P. GOTTSCHALK (1986) "Social programs—a partial solution to, not a cause of poverty: an alternative to Charles Murray's view," in Losing Ground: A Critique. IRP Special Report No. 38. Madison, WI: Institute for Research on Poverty.

DEJONG, G. (1983) "Defining and implementing the independent living concept," in N. Crewe and I. Zola (eds.) Independent Living for Disabled People. San Francisco: Jossey-Bass.

DESCHWEINITZ, K. (1975) England's Road to Social Security. South Bruswick, NY: A.S. Barnes.

"Directory of Independent Living Programs." (n.d.) Independent Living Research Utilization Project. Houston, TX.

Disability Rights Education and Defense Fund (D.R.E.D.F.) (1985) Disability Rights Review. Berkeley, CA: Author.

DUNCAN, O.D. (1985) Poverty: A Ten Year Review. Ann Arbor, MI: Institute for Social Research.

FABRICANT, M. (1985) "The industrialization of social work practice." Social Work (September): 12-19.

FABRICANT, M. (1986) "Creating survival services." Administration and Social Work (Fall).

FABRICANT, M. and S. BURGHARDT (1986) "Radical social work practice," in The Encyclopedia of Social Work.

FABRICANT, M. and I. EPSTEIN (1984) "Legal and welfare rights advocacy: complementary approaches in organizing on behalf of the homeless." Urban and Social Change Rev. (Winter).

FABRICANT, M. and M. KELLY (1986) "The political economy of homelessness." Catalyst (Fall).

FAY, F. (1977) "Problems of the severely and multiply handicapped," in White House Conference on Handicapped Individuals. Washington, DC.

FELDSTEIN, M. (1977) "Facing the crisis in social security." The Public Interest 47 (Spring): 90.

FERGIN, S. (1985) "Sicker and quicker." Village Voice (August 14): 17.

FLYNN, K. (1985) "The toll of deinstitutionalization," in P. Brickner et al. (eds.) Health Care of the Homeless People. New York: Springer.

Food Monitor (1979) "Emergency food centers' how-to." (July-August): 17.

FREIRE, P. (1971) Pedagogy of the Oppressed. New York: Seabury.

GOLDEN, G. (1980) Wealth and Poverty. New York: Bantam.

GOODWIN, L. (1985) The Social Psychology of Welfare. Washington, DC: Heath.

GOUGH, I. (1979) The Political Economy of the Welfare State. London: Macmillan.

HAYES, B. (1985) Speech delivered to the Interfaith Council of Union County, New Jersey, New Providence, NJ, October.

HOLMES NORTON, E. (1985) "Restoring the traditional black family." New York Times (June 2): 79.

HOPE, M. and J. YOUNG (1984) "From backwards to back alleys: deinstitutionalization and the homeless." Urban and Social Change Rev. (Summer).

HOPPER, K. and J. HAMBERG (1984) The Making of America's Homeless from Skid Row to New Poor, 1945-1984. New York: Community Service Society.

HORNBLUM, A. (1985) "New councils organize the jobless." In These Times (January 16-22): 3.

HOROWITZ, M., I. LAY et al. (1984) The State, the People and the Reagan Cuts: an Analysis of Social Spending Cuts. Washington, DC: A.F.S.C.M.E.

JOE, T. and C. ROGERS (1985) By the Few for the Few. Lexington, MA: Lexington.

JOHNSON, P. and A. RUBIN (1983) "Case management in mental health: a social work domain?" Social Work (January-February).

KOTELCHUK, R. (1985) "The effect of DRGs on health care." Health-Pac Bulletin (January): 7-14.

LADNER, J. (1986) "Teen-age pregnancy: the implications for black Americans," pp. 65-84 in The State of Black America. New York: National Urban League.

LANDO, M. et al. (1982) 1978 Survey of Disability and Work, U.S. Department of Health and Human Services. Washington, DC: Social Security Administration Office of Policy.

LAUFFER, A. (1985) Grantsmanship. Beverly Hills, CA: Sage.

LEEPSON, M. (1982) The Homeless: Growing National Problem. Washington, DC: Congressional Quarterly.

LELYVELD, J. (1985) "Hunger in America." New York Times Magazine (June 16): 53.

LEOFF, H. (1971) Appalachia's Children: the Challenge of Mental Health. Lexington: Univ. of Kentucky.

LEUCHTENBERG, W. (1963) Franklin Roosevelt and the New Deal. New York: Harper and Row.

LEWIS, O. (1959) Five Families: Mexican Case Studies in the Culture of Poverty. New York: Random House.

LEWIS, O. (1965) La Vida: a Puerto Rican Family in the Culture of Poverty. New York: Random House.

LIEBOW, E. (1957) Talley's Corner. New York: Rand McNally.

LOWRY, G. (1986) "Beyond civil rights," pp. 163-172 in the State of Black America. New York: National Urban League.

MOOM, M. and I. SAWHILL (1984) "Family incomes," pp. 317-346 in J. Palmer and I. Sawhill (eds.) The Reagan Record. Cambridge, MA: Ballinger.

MURRAY, C. (1982) Losing Ground. New York: Basic.

MYERS, J. (1981) "Social Security: myth and reality." Working Papers (July-August): 23-31.

National Unemployed News (1984) "The fight against mortgage foreclosures."
    Vol. 2, 1.
National Unemployed News (1984) "New unemployed committees: the why and
    how." Vol. 2, 1.
NEUGARTEN, B. (1982) "Age or need?" National Forum (Fall): 25-27.
New York Times (1984) "Goldin finds errors in welfare reporting." (February
    17): B23.
New York Times (1985) "Low-paying jobs foreseen for most working women."
    (February 12): A20.
New York Times (1985) "Doctors say hunger is epidemic in U.S." (February
    27): A12.
New York Times (1985) "Union strikes at all-time low." (September 1): 17.
New York Times (1985) "Massachusetts workfare program cited for success."
    (November 18): A27.
New York Times (1986) "Reagan plans restructuring of welfare program." (Feb-
    ruary 23): A24.
New York Times (1986) "Government panel finds Medicare fund solvent until
    end of century." (March 29): A16.
NOBLE, K. (1985) "Family faces grim life as jobless benefits gain." New York
    Times (April 6): A27.
Nutrition Watch (1982) Findings on Nutrition. (pamphlet)
OBERMANN, C. E. (1965) A History of Vocational Rehabilitation in America.
    Minneapolis, MN: T.S. Dennison.
OLSON, L. K. (1982) The Political Economy of Aging. New York: Columbia
    Univ.
PEARCE, D. (1978) "The feminization of poverty: women, work and welfare."
    Urban and Social Change Rev. (February).
PILIAVIN, I. (1985) "The 1965-1970 crime increase as seen by Charles Mur-
    ray: a critique," in Losing Ground: A Critique. IRP Special Report No. 38.
    Madison, WI: Institute for Research on Poverty.
PIVEN, F. and R. CLOWARD (1972) Regulating the Poor. New York: Vintage.
President's Task Force on Hunger (1985) Summary of Draft Final Report. Wash-
    ington, DC: Government Printing Office.
REINHOLD, R. (1985) "Energy recession ends Texas population boom." New
    York Times (October 21): A18.
REISSMAN, F. (1984) "Self-help and empowerment." Social Policy (Sep-
    tember-October): 3.
RICH, S. (1984) "Trimming disabled roles still raises furor." Washington Post
    (May 14).
ROMER, J. (1984) "Disability reform legislation becomes law," in Washington
    Watchline. Washington, DC: National Easter Seals Society.
ROTHSCHILD, E. (1981) "Reagan and the real America." The New York
    Review of Books (February).
SALERNO, D., K. HOPPER, and E. BAXTER (1984) Hardship in the Heart-
    land: Homelessness in Eight U.S. Cities. New York: Community Service
    Society.
SHECTER, S. (1982) Women and Male Violence: The Vision and Struggles of
    the Battered Women's Movement. Boston: South End.
SHIFREN-LEVINE, I. (1984) "Service programs for the homeless mentally
    ill," in R. Lamb (ed.) The Homeless Mentally Ill. Washington, DC: Ameri-
    can Psychiatric Association.

STALLARD, K., B. EHRENREICH, and H. SKLAR (1983) Poverty in the American Dream: Women and Children First. Boston: South End.

STERN, M. J. (1984) "The emergence of the homeless as a public problem." Social Service Rev. (June).

STONE, D. (1984) The Disabled State. Philadelphia: Temple Univ. Press.

STONER, M. R. (1984) "An analysis of public and private sector provisions for homeless people." Urban and Social Change Rev. (Winter).

SWENYARD, C. et al. (1977) "Rehabilitation and treatment," in White House Conference on Handicapped Individuals. Washington, DC: Government Printing Office.

THOMPSON, E. P. (1963) The Making of the English Working Class. New York: Pantheon.

THOMPSON, G. (1978) "Pension coverage and benefits in 1972: findings from the retirement history study." Social Security Bulletin 41 (February): 3-17.

TRATTNER, W. (1974) From Poor Law to Welfare State. New York: Free Press.

Urban Institute (1984) The Reagan Record. Cambridge, MA: Ballinger.

U.S. Bureau of the Census (1984a) Current Population Reports: Money Income of Households, Families and Persons in the U.S., 1982. Washington, DC: Government Printing Office.

U.S. Bureau of the Census (1984b) "Projections of the population of the U.S. by age, sex and race, 1983-2080." Current Population Reports, Series p. 25, no. 95. Washington, DC: Government Printing Office.

U.S. Bureau of Labor Statistics (1984) Employment and Earnings. Washington, DC: Government Printing Office.

U.S. Bureau of Labor Statistics (1985) Wages and Hours by Industry. Washington, DC: Government Printing Office.

U.S. Department of Health, Education and Welfare, Bureau of Family Services (1962) Work Relief: a Current Look. Public Assistance Report 52. Washington, DC: Author.

U.S. News and World Report (1984) "How much hunger is there in America?" (January 23): 35-36.

Village Voice (1985) "New York state embraces workfare programs." (October 14): 3.

WHITE, R. et al. (1981) High Quality Vocational Training for Welfare Women. Washington, DC: Bureau of Social Science Research.

WHITE, T. (1984) "The new war with Japan." New York Times Magazine (August 19): 66.

WOODY, B. and M. MAISON (1985) Crisis: Low Income Black Employed Women in the U.S. Workplace. Wellesley: Wellesley College Institute of Working Women.

Working Women, National Association of Office Workers (1980) Race against Time: Automation at the Office. Cleveland, OH: Author.

ABOUT THE AUTHORS

STEVE BURGHARDT is Associate Professor of Urban Policy and Practice at the Hunter College School of Social Work in New York. An activist since the 1960s, his work has centered on work in trade-union and community coalitions, international support work, and antiservice with networks. Author of numerous articles on organizing and the economic crisis, his books include *Tenants and the Urban Housing Crisis, The Other Side of Organizing* (Cambridge, Schenkman, 1982), and *Organizing for Community Action* (Newbury Park: Sage, 1982).

MICHAEL FABRICANT is Associate Professor of Urban Policy and Research at the Hunter College School of Social Work in New York. His books include *Deinstitutionalizing Delinquent Youth* (Schenkman, 1980) and *Juveniles in the Family Court* (Lexington: D. C. Heath, 1983). Author of numerous articles, the most recent of which are "The Industrialization of Social Work Practice" (*Social Work*, 1985), "The Political Economy of Homelessness" (*Catalyst*, 1986), and "Creating Survival Services" (*Administration and Social Work*, 1986), he has been an activist in the area of homelessness and is president of the Elizabeth Coalition to House the Homeless (an advocacy-organizing agency) as well as a board member at the National Coalition to House the Homeless.

NOTES

NOTES

NOTES

NOTES

362.509
B913w   Burghardt, Stephen

          Working under the
          safety net

DATE DUE

NOV 2 9 1992	NOV 25 '92		